El Camino de Costa Rica Hiking Guide

EVAN BRASHIER

Developed in partnership with
Asociación Mar a Mar
San José, Costa Rica

El Camino de Costa Rica Hiking Guide

Copyright © 2021 by Evan Brashier

First Edition, May 2021
All text, photographs, and maps by the author.

Edited by:
Asociación Mar a Mar
San José, Costa Rica
Executive Director: Conchita Espino, PhD

https://www.caminodecostarica.org/

Names: Brashier, Evan.
Title: El Camino de Costa Rica Hiking Guide / Evan Brashier
Description: First Edition. | San José, Costa Rica: Asociación Mar a Mar, 2021.
ISBN: 978-1-7371393-0-0 (color print) | 978-1-7371393-1-7 (ebook)
1. Hiking—Costa Rica—Guidebooks.
2. Camino—El Camino de Costa Rica—Hiking—Guidebooks.
3. El Camino de Costa Rica—Guidebooks.
4. Costa Rica—Travel— Hiking—Guidebooks.

Contents

Foreword

El Camino de Costa Rica takes hikers on a journey from the Atlantic to the Pacific, through the rural countryside of a splendid, diverse Central American nation. The trail features panoramic views of forested mountains, undulating farmland, and shimmering waters. People open their homes for travelers, and share the delights of local attractions and cultural traditions. This is what hikers can expect to encounter on the trail, in addition to shaded river valleys, cloud forests, mountain ridges that fade into the distance, colorful wildlife, and snapshots of an agricultural lifestyle that generates coffee, chocolate, and other produce enjoyed all over the world.

The fastest I have ever seen El Camino de Costa Rica completed was three days. Two runners embarked from Quepos, on the Pacific Coast of Costa Rica, and used their journey to raise funds for families in need. They ran through forests, villages, and mountain passes carrying only snacks and drinks, while I drove the support vehicle with their equipment. When they arrived at the dock in Muelle de Goshen, 68 hours later, we did what most people do to access the Caribbean Coast: we rode a ferry to the coastal islands, and walked down to the shore.

Along the trail, communities showed their support for the two athletes and provided them with rest stations, meals, and lodging for the few hours of sleep taken each night. People also donated to help families in the villages near El Camino de Costa Rica, especially those of women raising children alone. Witnessing this engagement, and the spirit of camaraderie and warmth among the local people, helped me understand the inspiration for the development of the hiking trail, and the vision of Asociación Mar a Mar, the organization that designed it: to bring attention to rural, inland regions of Costa Rica.

My first completion of El Camino de Costa Rica required a more moderate twelve days, as I was not available to drive alongside myself with my camping gear. But as I hiked and revisited the trail, and observed the variety of communities in different regions and elevations, I eventually understood that the destinations along the way were equally as important as the journey.

A meal enjoyed with a family at the end of a long day gains value if earned by hiking over a mountain first. Camping on a farm becomes immersive when accompanied by a tour from the owners and a sampling of dishes made from ingredients grown on their land. And experiencing a taste of the lives of the indigenous peoples of Costa Rica is intriguing, but only possible with a member of the tribe as a guide through their territory. With each subsequent crossing of El Camino de Costa Rica, I catalogued more experiences like these, and wanted others to have the same opportunity that I did to enjoy the trail.

That is why I wrote this guidebook: to facilitate your journey on El Camino de Costa Rica, from coast to coast, across a country and a continent. Written with support from Asociación Mar a Mar, this book focuses on distances, directions, and descriptions of what to expect so that you can navigate the route, set your schedule, and design your own adventure.

While developing this guide, I was served or hosted by several of the businesses and providers of lodging mentioned here, but always paid for their services. I did not receive discounts in exchange for their inclusion, or as an incentive to provide favorable comments. My hope is that this guidebook enables you to enjoy much of what I did on the trail, plus something new, in whichever direction, and at whatever pace, you choose. *Pura vida.*

– Evan Brashier

The author on the old bridge across Río Orosi: March of 2019

Introduction

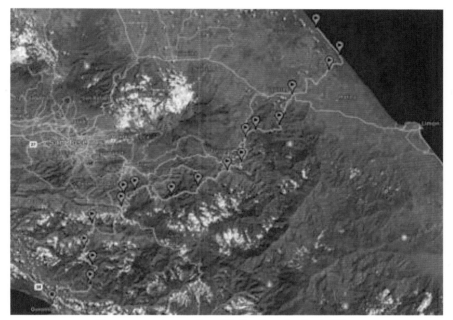

From coast to coast on El Camino de Costa Rica

About El Camino de Costa Rica

El Camino de Costa Rica begins at the Caribbean shore, north of the city of Limón, on coastal islands only accessible by air or sea. After we touch the water at the beach, ferries transport us along canals to the mainland. From there, the trail continues on land across Costa Rica to the town of Quepos, at the edge of the Pacific. Some stretches follow the sidewalk by national highways, and others trace narrow trails through dense jungles. There are creeks to cross, and mountains to climb. Two portions of the trail pass through protected territory, where a local guide is required. All other sections can be completed unaccompanied and without assistance.

About Asociación Mar a Mar

Asociación Mar a Mar is a non-profit organization based in Costa Rica that partners with Amigos of Costa Rica, its 501(c)(3) affiliate in the United States of America, to receive donations. It uses funds to: help local business owners market services to hikers; empower rural communities to serve tourists; and promote and maintain El Camino de Costa Rica. The goals of Asociación Mar a Mar are to:

- Provide tourists with a unique experience, and foster appreciation for the natural and cultural attractions of Costa Rica, by means of a maintained trail that unites the Atlantic and Pacific Oceans;
- Help the development of small rural businesses that demonstrate a commitment to sustainability;
- Offer destinations within rural communities that provide lodging, information, security, local gastronomic options, and other cultural attractions;
- Attract tourists who desire to walk the mountains, forests, valleys, and villages of Costa Rica, and appreciate its biodiversity;
- Mark the trail, and provide information for travel agencies and hikers; and,
- Generate employment in small communities through the establishment of guided tours for visitors who so desire them.

In recent years, Asociación Mar a Mar has contacted and collaborated with industry professionals, students, tourists, and tour guides, to establish the route and organize basic support and services along El Camino de Costa Rica. Organizational funds enable projects designed around:

- Helping communities improve their infrastructure and access to potable water, recycling, and other basic infrastructure as needed;
- Improving services for hikers, such as lodging, and providing exposure to or engagement with local cultures; and,
- Offering or facilitating guided tours.

The organization achieves its objectives by:

- Channeling funds, and serving as a catalyst for others to bring funds to development associations;
- Bringing volunteers to conduct or support small infrastructure projects; and,
- Promoting El Camino de Costa Rica, and bringing clients to rural entrepreneurs.

Independent hikers can contact Asociación Mar a Mar to receive current safety-related information and basic requirements in order to safely complete the route. Send requests to elcaminodecostarica@gmail.com or +506 6036-6199 on WhatsApp.

Getting to El Camino de Costa Rica

Basílica de Nuestra Señora de Los Ángeles in Cartago

Juan Santamaría International Airport

The main airport that serves Costa Rica is approximately 20 kilometers to the northwest of the capital, San José. Located in Alajuela, Juan Santamaría International Airport (SJO) receives direct flights from all over the world. The Costa Rica Greater Metropolitan Area (GAM) has expanded and now encompasses Alajuela, and buses and taxis frequently carry travelers between the airport and downtown San José. Since the hub for public transportation to other regions of Costa Rica is downtown, and buses do not operate past certain hours, we may spend a night in San José upon arrival. Regardless, if we intend to travel by bus to either end of El Camino de Costa Rica, we must first get from the airport to the city center.

From the airport, we can hire a taxi or take a bus to downtown San José. Taxis can deliver us directly to the appropriate bus terminal for transportation to El Camino de Costa Rica. The bus from the airport will get us close, but does not stop at the connecting terminals. If we ride this bus, we can walk from its last stop to another bus terminal, and continue from there. We can also take the bus into the city, and then use a taxi to go from terminal to terminal.

Before we leave the airport, we may want some of the local currency: *colones*. A few thousand would be useful for small transactions while on the way to either a bank or another establishment that can change money.

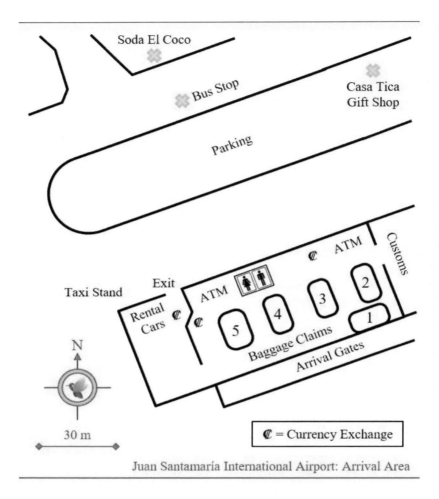

Juan Santamaría International Airport: Arrival Area

Inside the airport there are counters where currency can be exchanged to facilitate paying cash for transportation. Before leaving the city, it is prudent to have sufficient *colones* to pay not only for immediate needs, but also expenses for a few days. Not all towns on El Camino de Costa Rica have banks, which offer a better exchange rate than the airport, but businesses along the trail may not have the ability to receive payment by card. Thus, *colones* are often critical to avoid an exorbitant exchange rate imposed on payments in foreign currency.

Getting Around in San José

Taxi: Inside the baggage claim area of Juan Santamaría International Airport, or just outside it to the left, we can expect to find, or be approached by a representative from, the organized taxi service associated with the airport. Their distinct orange cars and vans are numbered, labelled, and metered to ensure standardized pricing. Taxis also feature yellow triangles on side doors, and yellow lights on top. The triangles and lights are consistent across Costa Rica, and inform passengers that a taxi operator is licensed and legitimate.

Beyond the local area surrounding the airport, and throughout the rest of Costa Rica, taxis are red. In most cities, there are designated taxi waiting areas. These are usually near other transit hubs, like bus terminals, or adjacent to central plazas. Red or orange, the taxis with yellow triangles and meters spare travelers the need to negotiate over a price. However, tipping drivers is appreciated.

Iglesia Nuestra Señora de La Merced, by La Merced Park in San José

Travel by taxi directly from San José to El Camino de Costa Rica only accommodates starting on the Pacific Coast, due to canals that prevent vehicles from accessing the trail at the edge of the Caribbean. However, the Pacific Coast trail terminus is approximately 150 kilometers from the airport, which should be considered when estimating the cost of a taxi. From the airport to the dock nearest the Caribbean start point of El Camino de Costa Rica is also approximately 150 kilometers.

Bus: The bus from Alajuela to downtown is big, red, and cheap compared to the price of a taxi. The bus stop is in front of the exit from the Juan Santamaría International Airport baggage claim area. To find the bus stop, we turn left just outside the airport door and walk 100 meters, past the row of taxis, on a street that curves to the right. We stop at the intersection and look to the right. The bus stop is clearly visible just down the street. We move to the waiting area, and watch for the red Tuasa bus that goes to the terminal at La Merced Park: Parada Alajuela.

Rental Vehicle: Several rental car agencies operate out of Juan Santamaría International Airport. With a rental vehicle, we can facilitate our own transportation to almost any point along El Camino de Costa Rica. However, this implies either using a support driver, or establishing a pattern of doubling back to retrieve the vehicle after covering sections of the trail. It also incurs the possibility of driving along roads that are not lit at night. The conditions of some roads are not represented accurately on driving aids (maps, GPS, etc.), which can incur safety risks and require turning back to find a different route. Due to these and other considerations, use of a rental vehicle is discouraged, and should only be undertaken after thorough risk analysis.

San José Bus Stations

Buses do not go directly from Juan Santamaría International Airport to either coast, or to any community along El Camino de Costa Rica. Therefore, when traveling by bus, hikers must ride from the airport to Parada Alajuela, and then transfer to one of two other bus stations in San José. Transfers are possible on foot, or in a taxi.

Parada Alajuela: Buses enter and then exit Parada Alajuela by driving in a counterclockwise arc through the terminal. The terminal itself is on the north side of Avenida 2, across from La Merced Park, at a 4-way intersection. At the opposite corner, Iglesia Nuestra Señora de La Merced towers above the trees. Inside the terminal, there are snack shops and pay-for-use bathrooms. The layout and traffic flow is as follows: buses enter from the east and offload, follow a curve to the south and load, then exit onto Avenida 2. Directly across from this exit, in the park, stands a bronze statue of Braulio Carrillo Colina, who led Costa Rica to independence from the Federal Republic of Central America in 1838.

If we arrive at Parada Alajuela on a bus from Juan Santamaría International Airport and intend to continue traveling by bus, there are two other bus stations in San José we will use. All three stations are within two kilometers of each other, and make three points of a triangle. We can either walk between them, or take quick taxi rides. To access the eastern start point of El Camino de Costa Rica, we use Terminal Caribeños. To start from the west coast, we use Bus Terminal Tracopa. These terminals are also where buses coming from those respective directions arrive.

Each bus station has a dominant color: Terminal Caribeños uses green

Terminal Caribeños: From the intersection with Parada Alajuela, La Merced Park, and Iglesia Nuestra Señora de La Merced, we walk north on Calle 12. This places Parada Alajuela on our left, with the park and the church behind us. At the first street that crosses Calle 12, a green street sign reads La Merced, and in smaller letters, Distrito 2. To our right, this is a pedestrian-only walkway. This road, also called Avenida Central, is paved with faded pink stones and lined with shops. We turn right onto this street, and walk east.

As we cross streets, paying close attention to streetlights and traffic at crosswalks, we observe that the street numbers decrease by two at each intersection, descending by the even numbers. Between Calle 4 and Calle 2, we identify a large kiosk of ATMs for Banco Nacional on our left. The next cross-street is Calle Central Alfredo Volio, or simply Calle Central. Here a decorated bull statue poses in the middle of the road. We turn left, and walk north on Calle Central, mindful to now use the sidewalk.

The streets that cross Calle Central increase in number by two at each intersection, starting with Avenida 1 and ascending by the odd numbers. When we reach Avenida 9, the terrain slopes down and offers a view of the northern mountains that border one side of the San José Greater Metropolitan Area. We continue on Calle Central, down the slope and across a bridge. On the far side of the bridge, the green brick fence that surrounds Terminal Caribeños comes into view on the left. Inside the terminal, we must proceed through the shopping corridor to find the ticket vendors at the far end. A column next to the ticket vendors reads Boletería, but the letters are only visible from directly in front of the vendor windows. We can also have a meal and buy food and some supplies at this station, although buses typically stop midway to Siquirres and Limón for a break at a rest area with a market.

Bus Terminal Tracopa: Based on the recommended east-to-west conduct of El Camino de Costa Rica, we depart San José for the Caribbean via Terminal Caribeños, and return from Quepos, which is by the Pacific. The bus from Quepos arrives in San José at Bus Terminal Tracopa, so from there we must return to Parada Alajuela for a connection to Juan Santamaría International Airport. We can also hire a taxi from Bus Terminal Tracopa and travel to the airport directly.

A blue fence surrounds the waiting area at Bus Terminal Tracopa, and matches the blue and white paint on the interior bricks. Taking the pedestrian exit, we step onto Calle 5 and turn right to face north. Taxi drivers offer their services, or we can walk to Parada Alajuela if we first continue north on Calle 5. The streets that cross Calle 5 decrease in even numbers by two at each intersection, starting with Avenida 18. Between Avenida 6 and Avenida 4, we see Parque de las Garantías Sociales on our right. We cross Avenida 2, and then pass Teatro Nacional de Costa Rica and Plaza de la Cultura on our left. This brings us to Avenida Central, where we turn left.

Walking west on Avenida Central, we pass a small clock tower that stands in the middle of the road. The Tourist Information Office appears on our left, and then we encounter a decorated bull statue in the street. As we continue, the street numbers increase by two at each intersection, ascending by even numbers. At Calle 12, we turn left, and arrive at the intersection with Parada Alajuela, La Merced Park, and Iglesia Nuestra Señora de La Merced. From Parada Alajuela, we can take a bus to the airport. To ensure that the bus will deliver us to the destination we desire, we can ask the driver, "Al aeropuerto?"

West-to-East Route: To conduct El Camino de Costa Rica from west to east, using bus transportation to access the trail, we can reverse the previous directions between the San José terminals, and depart from Bus Terminal Tracopa to Quepos. From Parada Alajuela to Bus Terminal Tracopa, we walk east on Avenida Central to Calle 5 and turn right. We proceed south on Calle 5 past Avenida 18, and enter the terminal near the large blue fence on our left. Returning from the Caribbean, we exit Terminal Caribeños and turn right to walk south on Calle Central. When we arrive at Avenida Central, we turn right and continue west down the pedestrian-only road to Calle 12. At Calle 12, we turn left, and arrive at the intersection with Parada Alajuela, La Merced Park, and Iglesia Nuestra Señora de La Merced. From Parada Alajuela, we can take a bus to the airport. To ensure that the bus will deliver us to the destination we desire, we can ask the driver, "Al aeropuerto?"

Start Points

Barra de Parismina (East): The recommended direction of travel along El Camino de Costa Rica is from east to west, starting in Limón Province at Barra de Parismina, an island on the Caribbean Coast. This sequences the more logistically challenging sections of the trail near the beginning. Reaching the coast requires traveling to islands not accessible via ground. There are not even bridges that lead to the coast. Then, Section 3 and Section 4, which lead to Río Pacuare, cannot be conducted without a guide from the local indigenous tribe.

Beyond Río Pacuare, we can move independently until Section 10, which also requires a hired guide. The elevation gradually increases to the high point of the trail, which is near Cerro Alto: this translates to "high hill." The remaining sections descend to Quepos. The bus station in Quepos offers regular rides to Bus Terminal Tracopa in San José, and from there the airport is 20 kilometers away by taxi.

Quepos (West): The western starting point of El Camino de Costa Rica is the town of Quepos, on the Pacific Coast, in Puntarenas Province. Starting here incurs a steeper ascent to Cerro Alto. It also increases the challenge of meeting a local guide at the indigenous territory border. From the west, the trail does not enter tribal land near a village located next to both a road and a nearby office of the local Parque Nacional.

From the west, arriving at the canals from which we access coastal islands is as simple as walking to the dock. However, leaving the islands and returning to San José requires either a ferry ride or flight, and a sequence of taxi and / or bus rides. While feasible, this process makes finishing the trail and getting home from the Caribbean much more complex than just arriving in Quepos, walking to the bus station, and taking a single bus to the capital. This is why hiking east-to-west is recommended.

Getting to Barra de Parismina

The community of Barra de Parismina can only be reached via flight or boat. No roads or bridges connect the island to the mainland. Swimming is prohibited by environmental protection policies, and is dangerous due to the wildlife.

Air: Regular flights to Barra de Parismina do not exist. There is not even a local tower for air traffic control. Flights to the island are typically coordinated as part of a fishing vacation package at Río Parismina Lodge. Incorporating this into conduct of El Camino de Costa Rica is possible, but expensive.

Water: A ferry passes between Barra de Parismina and the nearest dock on the mainland at multiple times throughout the day. The ride is five kilometers down a twisting canal, and should only take 15 minutes at the most. Ferry operators expertly negotiate sand bars in the canal, but do not provide many frills. This is public transportation, not a nature cruise. It is possible to arrange for private transportation along these waterways, but the cost increases. A seat on the public ferry costs 1500 *colones*. The white fiberglass boat has a solid roof, seating for 18 passengers, and large open portals from which to view the scenery.

The airstrip on Barra de Parismina

The mainland dock for the public ferry to Barra de Parismina is adjacent to Restaurante Caño Blanco, which sits at the end of Route 806, in the community for which the restaurant is named. However, reaching Caño Blanco from the nearest city, Siquirres, requires changing buses unless a taxi or personal transportation, such as a rental vehicle, was used to travel from San José.

Siquirres

The bus from Terminal Caribeños in San José that arrives in Siquirres stops at Gran Terminal del Caribe. From here, we can walk to the other bus station in town, or to the adjacent taxi stand. There are also several local shops and restaurants, which makes this a good place to buy food or supplies before embarking on the trail. Lodging options are limited, and outside the city. A taxi is the most efficient way to reach them. The village of Cimarrones, where homestays are available on the trail, is only 10 kilometers further east, along Route 32.

Walking out of Gran Terminal del Caribe, we see the town plaza diagonally across the intersection to our right. To reach the center of town, we turn right, cross Avenida 4, and proceed with the park on our left. The next street is Avenida 2, and once we cross that, we can find the local bus station on the left and the taxi stand on the right.

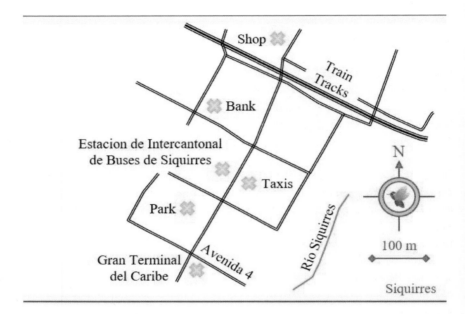

The local bus station is inside a large, unmarked bay with multiple stalls. The station can be identified on some maps as Estacion de Intercantonal de Buses de Siquirres. A center island guides the flow of traffic. Tickets are sold at the booth adjacent to the Comida Rapida del Atlantico, by the entrance to the covered bay. Buses leaving here for Restaurante Caño Blanco are scheduled to arrive there in concert with the ferry schedule. The ferry operators wait for the bus drivers, and the bus drivers wait for the ferry operators, which provides a coordinated and unified public service.

Taxis are available for hire across the street from the bus station, and travel the road to Restaurante Caño Blanco much faster than any bus. The drive is approximately 36 kilometers along a road of pavement and gravel, some of which is in very poor condition.

Upon arrival at Restaurante Caño Blanco, there is a large covered deck with pay-for-use bathrooms and a snack shop that operates around the ferry schedule. Restaurante Caño Blanco also provides a supervised, enclosed parking area behind the deck. Rental vehicles can be left overnight, for a fee of 5000 *colones* per night.

On Río Madre de Dios near the Caribbean Coast

Getting to Quepos

The coastal city of Quepos can be accessed via a single bus ride from Bus Terminal Tracopa in San José. For details on walking from the bus terminal in Quepos to El Camino de Costa Rica, refer to the description of Section 16.

Planning and Preparation

Before starting a journey on El Camino de Costa Rica, hikers are encouraged to research the area and the conditions, to prepare for a safe, relaxing experience. There are risks, but there are also resources, tools, and techniques available to mitigate those risks. This section addresses some ways in which hikers can prepare themselves and safely enjoy their travels along the trail.

Fitness: Consult with a physician before starting any exercise routine.

El Camino de Costa Rica is a trail for hiking, and does not require technical climbing or equipment like ropes and harnesses. Therefore, preparatory exercise plans should emphasize hiking up and down inclines of varying steepness, carrying equipment tailored to the journey. Leg, back, and core strength will help with weight management and balance, especially on the sections through forests, where the path is often wet, slick mud. Flexibility, and strong stabilization muscles around the lower joints, can reduce the risk of injury from slides, slips, and falls.

The brilliant flower of the ginger plant

The distance covered each day is at the discretion of the hiker, but recommended section breaks typically occur every 10 to 20 kilometers. Hikers can develop the endurance to cover comparable distances, or plan for stops at different intervals based on personal schedules, interests, and experience levels.

Trail surfaces vary, and include the mud already mentioned along with pavement, gravel roads, and dirt tracks through farmland. Training in appropriate footwear can help reduce blisters and other ailments associated with walking long distances up and down inclines on these surfaces.

An hourglass tree frog, named for the hourglass shape on its back

Nutrition and Hydration: Both are important components of health and physical fitness, and hikers can anticipate these needs as well. A day on El Camino de Costa Rica often includes breakfast and dinner at a private home or other lodging, based on predetermined trail sections. Food and supplies in remote areas may be harder to find. Before departing, it is wise to estimate caloric needs and either pack suitable and sufficient food, or conduct analysis while in communities along the trail and shop accordingly, based on upcoming distances. To maintain hydration, a water filter or purifier reduces risk when drinking from local sources, of which there are many. Bottled water is available in most shops. Drinking untreated water from natural sources, or from the tap in remote areas, is not advised. In cities, tap water is potable.

Costa Ricans are familiar with dietary restrictions, and can accommodate vegetarian, vegan, and other diets and preferences if asked to do so. Please submit special requests to lodging providers in advance, so they can shop and prepare accordingly. Otherwise, meals eaten in private homes will consist of cultural staples.

Gear: Outside of suitable footwear and a tool for treating water, it is possible to complete El Camino de Costa Rica with a shockingly small pack. Through research and planning, hikers can find lodging at every stop along the trail. In some seasons, it is possible to hike for two weeks and never encounter more than a slight drizzle of rain. However, planning for these conditions and expecting nothing to deviate is not a recipe for success. Hikers are urged to select their gear in advance, and practice its employment before departing for Costa Rica. Recommended items include:

- A three-season tent, with a rain fly or similar shield or coating.
- A sleeping bag comfortable down to temperatures above freezing. At night in the higher elevations, the temperature can drop significantly.
- A waterproof jacket that can be worn comfortably while hiking.
- Long pants, to reduce exposure to insects, and to plants that have thorns or sharp edges. Long pants also provide protection from the sun.
- A navigational aid, like a GPS device. It is possible to download the trail onto certain devices, which is an option for hikers who will not have mobile internet connectivity. Electrical outlets provide 110 volts for flat, two-pronged plugs.

If internet access along the trail is desired, the recommended local provider is Claro. Modifications to personal electronic devices, such as the installation of a local SIM card, are at the discretion of the hiker. Consider consulting with regular service providers and the manufacturer prior to modifying personal electronics.

Coordination: Costa Rica is digitally connected. A wireless signal is available almost everywhere along El Camino de Costa Rica, if using a local network. The preferred methods of making contact with lodging providers are, in this order: WhatsApp, Messenger, email, and other websites that facilitate tourist accommodations. Some businesses also maintain their own websites.

Although the spontaneity of arriving in a village and finding a place to stay has its appeal, this will surprise homestay providers and put them in an unfair, awkward situation. Hotels and establishments that offer cabins can be more flexible with unexpected travelers, but they may also be full. Therefore, it is wise to coordinate evening lodging and meals at least in the morning on the anticipated day of arrival, and preferably a day or more in advance. When providers request arrival times, it is often to ensure meals are ready. At a homestay, food for guests is usually from the family dinner, so times help providers prepare and establish a schedule for other activities.

Another advantage of prior coordination for lodging is the potential to have transportation to a destination that is slightly off of the trail. This book provides directions and the contact information for some locations that are not directly adjacent to the trail, but the book cannot provide a vehicle for a hiker. A local provider may help to arrange rides. This expands the number and variety of sites available for lodging. Providers can also return hikers to the trail, and assist with coordinating other activities offered in the local area: tours, tastings, or side trips.

A local guide is required in the indigenous territory

Guides and Services: El Camino de Costa Rica passes through indigenous territory, where it is critical to be joined by a member of the local tribe. Based on their operations, tribal guides may have solo hikers form a group and hike together. Details on crossing the tribal area are outlined in Section 3 and Section 4.

Section 10 requires a guide through Palo Verde Reserva, a protected cloud forest in the mountains between Navarro del Muñeco and the town of Palo Verde. Contact information for guides is provided in Section 10 and in the references.

Prior coordination is also valuable when planning to access the coastal islands on the Caribbean. No roads connect these islands to the mainland. Some locations are serviced by regular public transportation, but others can only be visited by request, via a private ferry. With prior coordination, hikers can plan with ferry operators to secure transportation along the canals to these remote destinations.

Seasons: Rather than focus on traditional seasons in Costa Rican, hikers should consider rain and heat. The rainy season begins in May and ends in November. The hot, dry season begins in December and ends in April. However, these are generalizations. Seasons are not uniform across all regions and elevations.

During the rainy season in most of the country, the coast by the Caribbean remains hot and humid. Rain is more common in this region during the standard winter and summer months. Inland, in the mountains, the rainy season is characterized by daily showers that begin in the early afternoon and end in the evening. The severity varies, and can change from minute to minute. Gathering clouds are observable from great distances, allowing hikers to plan for safety and find shelter. Mornings during the rainy season are also hot, since the sun rises around 6:00 and immediately increases the humidity. Hikers may wish to start moving early, to cover ground before the temperature rises and reach their destinations before the rain begins.

When requested in advance, a ferry can arrive at any time, day or night

In the dry season, it is possible to experience several days without rain. This can reduce access to water along certain stretches of El Camino de Costa Rica, as intermittent streams in the hills vanish. Combined with the heat, this can contribute to a risk of dehydration. The risk can be mitigated by planning, and by carrying sufficient water containers and a water filter or purifier.

Protection from the sun is important regardless of the weather or season. Natural shade in some areas is limited, such as in farmland where crops do not grow very tall, and on paths that follow high ridges. Suitable clothes, like long pants, tops with long sleeves, and hats, can reduce the effects of exposure.

Duration: The pace at which hikers cover El Camino de Costa Rica is a personal choice. With adequate support and conditioning, it is possible to run the length of the trail in three days. Completing one designated section each day would require 16 days of hiking various distances, and this does not include time for travel to and from trail start and end points. It is also possible to combine sections, or design a timeline focused on specific interests or requirements. The recommended planning factor is two weeks: starting with this, hikers can forecast and coordinate lodging based on individual abilities and daily distance estimates.

Suggested Section Combinations

Section 3 & Section 4: These two sections traverse the indigenous territory, where a guide from the local tribe is required. Combining the two sections reduces the overall obligation for a local guide, whose primary occupation is likely not accompanying hikers. Since guides usually charge by the day, the combination can also reduce costs.

Section 10 & Section 11: The shorter distance of Section 10 is offset by the challenge of passing through a cloud forest on a rough, wet trail, even with the required guide in Palo Verde Reserva. Combining Section 10 with Section 11 creates a long ascent to Cerro Alto, but lodging near the end of either section provides a welcome respite when covered in mud, spider webs, and forest debris.

Section 14-16 (Various): Lodging in these sections is not consolidated around any central community hub. Thus, it is practical to finish these three sections in two days, with a single night at a convenient mid-point. There are many options of where to sleep, per the preference of the hiker. Section 16 concludes at the end of the trail in Quepos, so the motivation to finish can also reduce the effect of the distance and the pace.

A coatimundi tries to hide under a fallen tree

Guide to Section Descriptions

Método de Información de Excursiones (MIDE) Scale

The Método de Información de Excursiones (MIDE) method of rating trails is used by the Spanish Federation of Mountain Sports and Climbing (FEDME) and Montaña Segura to measure four different trail characteristics: risks of the environment, complexity of trail navigation, difficulty of movement, and amount of effort required. Difficulty grades associated with mountaineering, such as those established by the International Climbing and Mountaineering Federation (UIAA), do not provide the detail necessary to describe El Camino de Costa Rica, which can be completed entirely without ropes or technical climbing equipment. Using MIDE ratings enables hikers to anticipate the specifics of each trail section, and prepare accordingly.

Risks of the Environment	1. Not free of risks
	2. A few risk factors
	3. Some risk factors
	4. Several risk factors
	5. Many risk factors
Complexity of Trail Navigation	1. Well-defined roads and crossings
	2. Paths or signs indicating continuity
	3. Identification of terrain references required
	4. Navigation outside the traced route required
	5. Navigation blocked by obstacles
Difficulty of Movement	1. Flat surfaces
	2. Dirt tracks
	3. Staggered paths and irregular terrain
	4. Use of hands required for balance
	5. Use of hands required for progression
Amount of Effort Required	1. Up to 1 hour of moving
	2. Between 1 and 3 hours moving
	3. Between 3 and 6 hours moving
	4. Between 6 and 10 hours moving
	5. More than 10 hours moving

Trail Conditions

The trail consists mainly of packed dirt or gravel roads, paved streets, and paths through fields and farmland. Some sections require passage through dense jungles, where river crossings, narrow routes, steep slopes, and thick vegetation prevent vehicle access. Along some sections the terrain includes significant elevation changes.

Trail Markers and Blazes

Trail markers take one of three forms. The most common is a short, red horizontal line above a white horizontal line of the same length. These appear at varying heights, painted on rocks, trees, fenceposts, street signs, and other surfaces. A red or white hummingbird is common at intersections and turns, with the beak pointing in the direction of travel. Hard signs with the logo of Asociación Mar a Mar are more rare.

El Camino de Costa Rica is marked with red and white blazes

A hummingbird marks the platform at Muelle de Goshen

Be alert and judicious when evaluating trail markers: other trails marked with similar colors cross, intersect, or overlap El Camino de Costa Rica, but Asociación Mar a Mar only uses the three marking types described here. If in doubt, refer to the maps, images, and location descriptions provided in this book.

Pictures and Text

The written directions and descriptions of El Camino de Costa Rica outline each section from east to west. Measurements are provided according to the metric system, which is the standard in Costa Rica. Due to fluctuations in connectivity and device performance, distances are approximate to within 100 meters. Pictures of local areas, sites, specific perspectives, and trail markings can aid in navigation.

The photographs in section descriptions depict areas mentioned in the nearby text. All were taken from or near the trail. However, some images reflect travel from west to east, often to highlight a specific landmark. Buildings may change color, or be demolished or improved upon, and no longer match the pictures in the book. The natural environment in Costa Rica also changes with time, due to development, conservation, farming, and land management. And, it should be noted that there are several pictures of forested mountain slopes, which may be difficult to distinguish.

Map Legend

Maps in this book are for reference purposes only: they are not sufficiently detailed to use for navigation if lost. The maps, text, and pictures here are intended to help a hiker orient to and remain on the trail. All data was accurate at the time of publication.

▶	Section Start Point
◼	Section End Point
�	Point of Interest
⌂	Lodging
━ ━ ➤	Trail (with Direction of Travel)
 ═══	Road (Any Surface)
≡≡≡	Train Tracks
▬▬▬	Border or Boundary
──	River, Canal, or other Waterway
▣	Contained Body of Water
⌒⌒⌒	Ocean or Sea
··········	Alternate Route

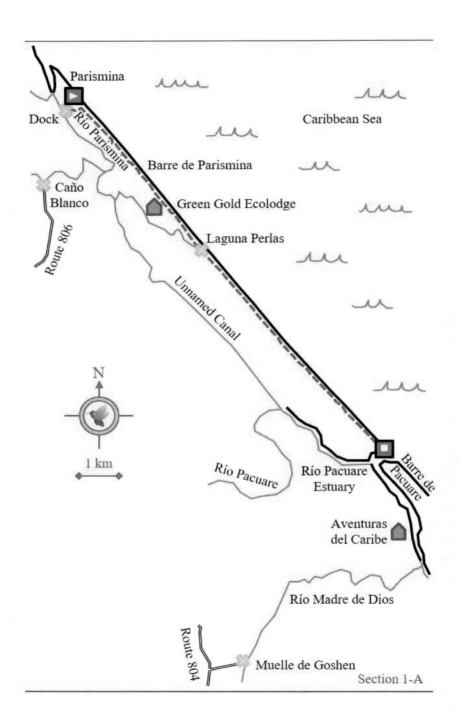

Parismina

Dock

Caribbean Sea

Río Parismina

Barre de Parismina

Caño Blanco

Green Gold Ecolodge

Route 806

Laguna Perlas

Unnamed Canal

N

1 km

Río Pacuare

Río Pacuare Estuary

Barre de Pacuare

Aventuras del Caribe

Río Madre de Dios

Route 804

Muelle de Goshen

Section 1-A

30

Section 1-A: Barra de Parismina – Muelle de Goshen

A distant fishing boat on the Caribbean at sunrise, near Parismina

The first section of El Camino de Costa Rica includes coastal islands that cannot be reached by roads, but are the only place to touch the Caribbean and begin a complete crossing of the country. The beaches in this area provide nesting grounds for several turtle species, all of which are protected by the government. At night, beach access is restricted, but watching the sunrise from the edge of the trees provides an inspiring start to a hike along the coast.

1	2	2	2	Distance: 12.7 km / 7.9 mi
				Estimated Walk Time: 2 hr, 40 min
				Total Elevation Gain: 80 m / 262 ft
				Total Elevation Loss: 81 m / 266 ft

8 m

0 m

0   3.2   6.4   9.5   12.7 km

The dock at Parismina, seen from the public ferry as it approaches

Km 0: Barra de Parismina (Northern End)

This section requires traveling along canals, but not all water access points are serviced by public transportation. Therefore, prior coordination is required to facilitate transfers between some locations. Based on time, cost, and ferry availability, we may choose to omit some parts of this section. The objective is to reach the coast, hike down to the water of the Caribbean, and truly begin El Camino de Costa Rica at the shore. There are multiple sites where we can accomplish this, but the preferred location is near the village of Parismina, directions to which appear earlier in this book.

The ferry from Restaurante Caño Blanco delivers us to a concrete dock on the inland side of the island of Barra de Parismina. We step onto a road of firm grey sand. The restaurant Rancho La Palma, to our right, offers meals under a covered dining space. We follow the road straight ahead to a T-intersection. The perpendicular road is one of three sandy paths that form a rough triangle around the village of Parismina, the longest side of which only measures 300 meters. Many of the local resources are found on these roads. We turn right and begin following this side of the triangle.

After our right turn onto the triangle, we spot the Subdelegacion Policial de Parismina on our left, and continue straight to a blue station for the Acueductos y Alcantarillados (AyA), also on our left. We turn left around this station, onto the next side of the triangle. After 100 meters, we see a church on the left. Another

100 meters brings us to a pulperia painted with red, yellow, and green stripes similar to the flag of Bolivia. A playground is on the opposite side of the street.

A vibrant mural of coastal life decorates a shop in Parismina

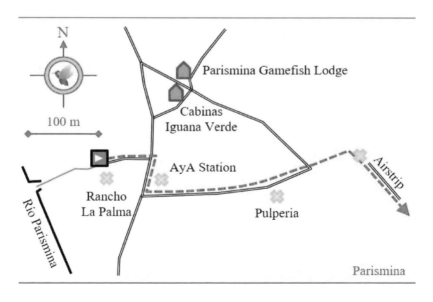

At the next intersection, we can turn left onto the third side of the triangle through the village, or continue straight to the northern end of an airstrip. Parismina Gamefish Lodge is down the road to the left, across from the Cabinas Iguana Verde and a restaurant, but our route is straight ahead.

A large number 14 is painted in white letters at the northern end of the airstrip, which we follow to the south. Rather than walk on the paved landing surface, where the temperature is higher, we use a path in the grass on the right. This track runs parallel to the airstrip for 1 kilometer, past small farms and a cemetery, before entering the trees. We leave the airstrip behind and continue straight along the green corridor through the forest, under a thick, leafy canopy.

From where we entered the trees at the end of the airstrip, we have 2.2 kilometers to cover before arriving at the gate to Green Gold Ecolodge. The trail here consists of the same grey sand as the beach, and is protected from the sun by the trees, except for a few exposed patches. At these areas, we move parallel to the shore, and reconnect with the trail under the trees on the far edge of the clearings. Narrow side trails lead inland to farms tucked among the trees, but we ignore these.

A manicured path through the gardens at Green Gold Ecolodge

Km 3.7: Green Gold Ecolodge

South of the village of Parismina, only Green Gold Ecolodge offers lodging on the island, but prior coordination is advised to ensure meals will be available. The staff can also provide tours of the on-site vanilla field, samples of coconuts and other fruit grown on the property, and assistance with night walks on the beach to search for turtles. Beach access at night is heavily regulated, and the Green Gold Ecolodge staff can ensure compliance with local policies. For example, the only light sources authorized on the beach at night are those with a red lens or bulb, which the staff can provide. Poachers are also active in the area, despite the efforts of the National Coast Guard Service, environmental scientists, and law enforcement agencies. This is why local assistance with beach visits increases safety for both tourists and the wildlife.

Looking north up the canal at Laguna Perlas

From Green Gold Ecolodge, we continue south on the trail through the trees for another 1.6 kilometers, to a wide clearing where a canal feeds into Laguna Perlas and sometimes spills into the sea. With prior coordination, a private ferry operator can meet us here and transport us south to Barra de Pacaure.

Km 5.3: Laguna Perlas

Without a ferry, we must continue on foot along the coast for an additional 7.4 kilometers, to the Río Pacuare estuary. As we pass Laguna Perlas, the tides and season may require wading through shallow water where the canal empties into the Caribbean. This may also be necessary in other areas where erosion has lowered the level of the sand. At the estuary, Río Pacuare is too deep to cross, but this spot is close to lodging options and the local Estacion de Guardacostas.

Km 12.7: Río Pacuare Estuary

From the estuary, we can only continue via pre-arranged ferry. Although it is possible to ride directly from the Río Pacuare estuary to Muelle de Goshen, we have the option of staying at local lodging and exploring Barra de Pacuare. Lirio Lodge, Reserva Pacuare, and Aventuras del Caribe all offer lodging and meals along Río Madre de Dios, which merges with Río Pacuare at the estuary. The staff at these locations can also arrange fishing trips, and provide tours of the canals to spot monkeys, crocodiles, bats, sloths, and other wildlife.

Fishing at the coast of the Caribbean, by the mouth of Río Pacuare

Julio, the manager of Aventuras del Caribe, can also facilitate a guided tour through Reserva Pacuare – the Pacuare Reserve – located on the coastal island to the east of Río Madre de Dios. A short ride across the canal from his cabins leads to the dock at the northern entrance of this nature sanctuary. From here, the cabins and workspaces used by volunteers and the Reserva Pacuare staff are 500 meters towards the coast.

Reserva Pacuare

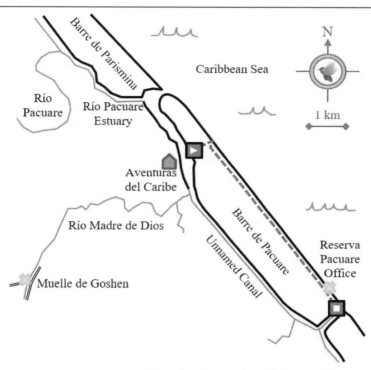

Río Pacuare

Barre de Parismina

Caribbean Sea

N

1 km

Río Pacuare Estuary

Aventuras del Caribe

Río Madre de Dios

Barre de Pacuare

Unnamed Canal

Reserva Pacuare Office

Muelle de Goshen

The optional route through Reserva Pacuare

⚠ 1	🧭 1	🍾 2	❤ 2	Distance: 6.6 km / 4.1 mi
				Estimated Walk Time: 1 hr, 20 min
				Total Elevation Gain: 15 m / 49 ft
				Total Elevation Loss: 16 m / 52 ft

23 m

1 m

| 0 | 1.6 | 3.3 | 4.9 | 6.6 km |

Scientists and guests at the Reserva conduct and observe research on the local turtle population, and witness the cycle of nesting and hatching. Reserva Pacuare also provides a home for several hundred other animal species, which we may observe while traversing the island from north to south on a shaded trail by the sand.

Looking across Río Madre de Dios to Aventuras del Caribe

Turning south near the Reserva Pacuare cabins, we follow a trail parallel to the coast for 5.8 kilometers. Since this is a private facility, Julio or a staff member will join us. The environment is similar to what we encountered on Barra de Parismina. Near the southern end of the path, we pass the headquarters of the Pacuare Reserve. Here, specialists and displays provide information about the efforts to protect turtles that nest on the island. At the southern tip of the island, a sign that warns of crocodiles signifies our return to the canals. The presence of these and other animals, and the fragility of the environment, necessitates caution inside the Pacaure Reserve and on the water.

Km 19.3: Southern End of Barra de Pacuare (Optional)

From the southern end of Barra de Pacuare, we require a ferry to travel along Río Madre de Dios to the dock at Muelle de Goshen. The ride is almost 12.5 kilometers, including a long, straight stretch on the western side of the Pacuare Reserve. This can take 30 minutes or more, but provides another opportunity to spot wildlife in the Cariari National Wetlands. Barra de Pacuare is not serviced by regular ferry providers, but the lodging companies in the area can coordinate transportation from local boat operators, regardless of whether we stay at their facilities.

Looking across Río Madre de Dios from Aventuras del Caribe

Once we arrive at Muelle de Goshen and step onto the concrete dock, El Camino de Costa Rica continues across the entire country to Quepos without the need for another boat.

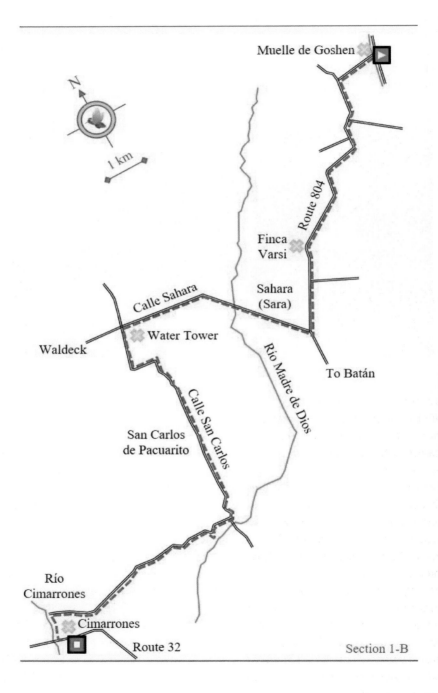

Muelle de Goshen

Route 804

Finca Varsi

Calle Sahara

Sahara (Sara)

Waldeck

Water Tower

Río Madre de Dios

To Batán

Calle San Carlos

San Carlos de Pacuarito

Río Cimarrones

Cimarrones

Route 32

Section 1-B

1 km

N

Section 1-B: Muelle de Goshen – Cimaronnes

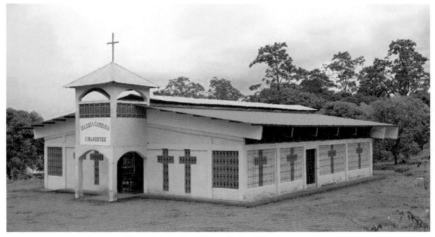

The Catholic Church in Cimarrones

Leaving the coastal islands, we cross a broad, flat, tropical lowland dedicated to pastures for livestock and industrial agriculture. Banana plantations, farms, and fields line our path until we approach villages near National Primary Route 32. Although there is little gain of elevation in this section, the lack of shade still makes water a valuable commodity. Fortunately, shops along the way sell food and cold drinks. We conclude just beyond the train tracks that connect San José and Limón, in the community of Cimarrones.

⚠ 2	🧭 2	🥾 1	❤ 3	Distance: 23.5 km / 14.6 mi
				Estimated Walk Time: 4 hr, 50 min
				Total Elevation Gain: 95 m / 312 ft
				Total Elevation Loss: 24 m / 79 ft

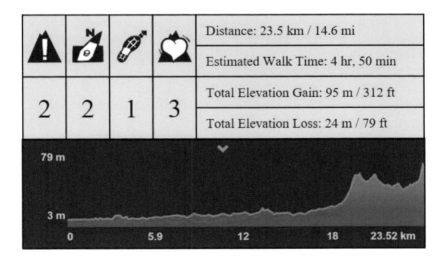

The shaded canal leading to Muelle de Goshen

Km 0: Muelle de Goshen

The Spanish word for "dock" is *muelle*, and Muelle de Goshen is the dock where boats from Barra de Pacuare retrieve and deliver their passengers. The structure consists of a concrete boat ramp and a covered waiting area with shaded benches. Across a dirt road, the enclosed compound provides a supervised parking area for guests of Lirio Lodge. The actual Lodge is located near Barra de Pacuare, one of several hospitality options near the coast.

Starting at the boat ramp, facing away from the canal, we make a U-turn to the right and cross the canal on a small bridge. For the first kilometer, we proceed along a narrow gravel and dirt road with dense vegetation on both sides. At the intersection with a wider gravel road, a sign for Lirio Lodge points back down the road we just covered. The broader road is Route 804. Cargo trucks use this road to move goods back and forth between the major highway that connects Limón to San José, and the plantations and communities along the coast. We turn left onto Route 804, and walk south. Due to the potholes in the dirt, drivers maneuver freely across the road, so we exercise caution, walk facing traffic, and listen for vehicles from behind us.

Route 804 passes through vast fields and farmland

After 600 meters, we pass the first rustic farm homes along Route 804, and follow the curve of the road to the right, past a bus stop at a minor intersection. Many homes and small farms have entrances along this road, but we ignore them and walk alongside the cattle pastures. Cows often rest in the shade from trees growing along the barbed wire fences that line Route 804. They give us little attention. One kilometer past the bus stop, we walk along a canal that separates the homes on our left from the main road. Then the road curves to the left, and exposes us to the scale of the terrain, and the effects of time on a geologic scale. The distant ridges eroded over thousands of years as the Caribbean receded, and created the plains we now cross.

We follow the curves of the road for 1.8 kilometers, and cross several reinforced canals along the way. This brings us to the gate of the Finca Varsi plantation, and a curve to the left. Behind the high bushes on either side of the road, we see rows of banana trees with their crops sometimes wrapped in blue plastic, which protects the fruit from pests, and fosters growth. After 900 meters, a road intersects Route 804 from the left. A bus stop at the intersection offers shade, but we continue straight for another 1.2 kilometers. Here we reach a Y-intersection, and turn sharply back to the right onto a paved road that leads past a fence on the right. Route 804 continues to the south as a wide gravel road, but our paved path takes us into the village of Sahara. There is also a sign for Lirio Lodge here, with its arrow pointing back to the dock.

Km 7.5: Sahara (Sara)

Just 100 meters past the Y-intersection, we cross a concrete slab bridge. In another 300 meters, a dirt road leads into fields farmed by the people here, but we remain on the pavement and ignore such diversions. We pass the first village church, Iglesia Santidad Pentecostal, on our right after 300 meters, and then a second church 400 meters farther along on our left. The second church is across from the village sports field. Between the churches, most homes are small wooden structures in varying condition. Straight past the second church, the pavement transitions to a gravel road leading away from the village center. We enter a neighborhood of brick houses, many painted in bright solid colors. The community ends after 900 meters, as we cross a concrete slab bridge over Río Madre de Dios and then stay to the left at a Y-intersection.

The water tower at Waldeck

Beyond the bridge another 2.5 kilometers to the west, we arrive at a 4-way intersection with a bus stop on the far side of the street. Looking left, we spot a blue water tower 100 meters to the south, on the left side of the road. The tank atop the tower supports the local communities: hikers are prohibited from entering the chain link fence that surrounds it. We turn towards the water tower and follow the gravel road. In 700 meters, we enter a large banana plantation lined with concrete fence columns marked CBCR, for Compañia Bananera de Costa Rica. After a left turn 200 meters ahead, and another to the right after 500 more meters, we cross a canal and observe the vastness of this enterprise. Tall bushes border both sides of the road, and beyond them in every direction are banana trees. Along the horizon, the distant mountains at the edge of the Cordillera de Talamanca create a green ribbon of earth between the plantation and the sky.

Across the next 600 meters, the road follows an S-curve to the left and then the right. This leads us to a conveyer system that allows harvesters to move bananas on cables and rails from the fields to processing plants. It spares the farm workers from carrying banana bunches very far, and avoids bruising the bananas. If a banana train is moving to the warehouse, a farmer will lower a yellow rail across the road for others to slide their crops along the cables. It is best to stay clear of the conveyers when this happens, and wait for the rail to lift.

A concrete slab bridge crosses a stream not 200 meters beyond the banana conveyer. While on the bridge, a look through the trees to the left reveals one of the cables for the rail system crossing the waterway. After another 200 meters, we arrive at the northern end of a village for farm workers and their families to live inside the plantation. We continue straight through this community, past the colorful homes, on the wide gravel road guiding us towards the mountains. From the first of these houses, we walk 600 meters and reach a paved section of the road.

Bunches of bananas travel on cable and rail systems to warehouses for sorting

Km 15.0: San Carlos de Pacuarito

45

The 900 meters of pavement here delineate the beginning and end of San Carlos de Pacuarito. Just 100 meters into the village, we pass Pulperia Mis Niñas on our left, one of the places where we can purchase meals, other food, and drinks. Continuing along the pavement another 300 meters, we pass Abastecedor Doña Mirna to our right and the local clinic to our left. In the next 500 meters, we see the village school and Abastecedor Mami before crossing a concrete bridge over the petite San Carlos canal. The pavement ends, and the banana plantation closes in on both sides.

Another banana conveyer crosses the road 100 meters past the San Carlos canal. The processing plant and shipping station are directly to our right. The village for workers begins immediately beyond the plant and continues for 300 meters along the road. Neighborhoods of matching homes line the sports field to the left. Most shops and services are specifically for the people that live here, and are best avoided by us.

A set of long S-curves begins 400 meters past the plantation village. We veer right, then left, then right over 500 meters before reaching a T-intersection. Here we turn right and stay on the wide gravel road. Another 500 meters brings us to the first noticeable incline on this section, as the road curves uphill to the left. We ascend for 800 meters, following the road past homes with fences lined with flowering trees. The school for this community is on the right after 300 meters: Escuela Unión Campesina.

Past the school, we cover 1.5 kilometers before the next plantation. Pineapple shrubs grow in dark green rows that cover the terrain up the slope to the horizon on our right. Pastures to the left support grazing. The main gravel road curves to the left 300 meters past our first encounter with these pineapple fields, but we divert from it and continue straight on a dirt road between the crops and trees. In 100 meters, we bypass the access roads that lead into the fields and stay on the straight path to a stream crossing. Although the bridge has collapsed, we can walk through the shallow water and continue on the far side. Denser tree growth along the road provides overhead protection once we are 600 meters past this stream, and then we have our last view of pineapple fields.

After another 700 meters, the dirt road slopes down a riverbank and ends at the edge of Río Cimarrones. We take the grassy, narrow path along the bank to the left. This path follows the river to the south, on a route outlined by tire tracks. Taking the path, we avoid crossing the waterway. In 400 meters, we arrive at train tracks, with a metal railroad bridge immediately to our right. Local trains to and from Limón transit here regularly, so we cross with care and continue straight for 200 meters. This brings us up a small incline to National Primary Route 32.

Route 32 connects Limón to San José. Vehicles pass swiftly in both directions. We stay on the near side of the street, turn left, and walk facing traffic to the town of Cimarrones. A wide shoulder allows us to stay safely off of the road. In 200 meters, we arrive at a bus stop, the Iglesia Católica Cimarrones, and the end of this section.

The trail continues south, next to Río Cimarrones, to a train bridge

Km 23.5: Cimarrones

From outside the fence at Iglesia Católica Cimarrones, we can find lodging 100 meters down the slope that leads past the church, at the end of a short paved road. Taking this option, we find ourselves back at the train tracks, and can see the large metal bridge over Río Cimarrones to the left. The house on the corner, with the shrine in the yard, is Casa Yolanda. Yolanda and her husband Manuel can accommodate people in two guest rooms, and in their covered, enclosed garage. Casa Yolanda is conveniently located near the start of the next trail section. Yolanda provides meals, and Manuel is a driver who can facilitate transportation to and from Muelle de Goshen.

Another homestay option in Cimarrones is Casa Araña. From the church, we continue for 800 meters along Route 32, using a trail parallel to the main road for safety. When available, we use the sidewalk in front of the homes that line the road. When we pass the village sports field on our left, a concrete road turns left down the slope from Route 32. We make the turn, and see a fire hydrant in front of the wooden house on our right. Painted tires decorate the front of this home, which is surrounded by a tall chain link fence. Inside, there is a room for guests. Tents can be used outside, with the exterior fence as protection. This residence offers an internet connection, and is close to a small shop that sells food and drinks. To reach the shop, we continue down the paved side road 100 meters to the train tracks, and then turn left and follow the tracks for 100 meters. The store, a Pulperia, is on the right, across the tracks.

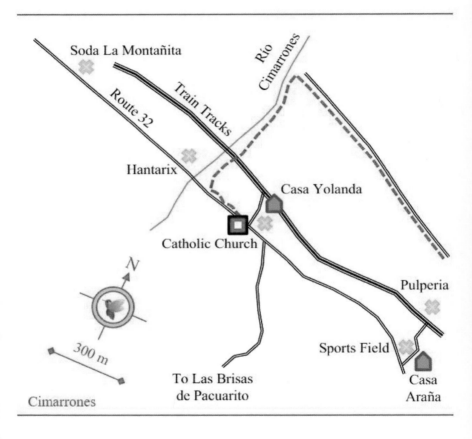

There are also two restaurants near Cimarrones, to the west along Route 32. Starting at Iglesia Católica Cimarrones, the first is Hantarix Del Caribe, 400 meters from the church, on the far side of Río Cimarrones. Hantarix features a dance hall, and serves as a local club. The second is Soda La Montañita, a popular stop for truckers and travelers along the road, 500 meters past Hantarix. It offers a selection of entrees all day, with ample seating.

The railroad bridge at Río Cimarrones: the trail crosses the tracks

Cimarrones to Barra de Pacuare: Casa Yolanda is a possible staging area from which to access the coastal islands. A bus from Terminal Caribeños in San José headed to Limón can deliver us to the bus stop adjacent to Iglesia Católica Cimarrones. The walk to Casa Yolanda from the bus stop is short. With coordination between Manuel and Julio, the manager of Aventuras del Caribe, we can ride from Casa Yolanda to Muelle de Goshen, and then catch a ferry to Barra de Pacuare. Julio can assist with a tour through Pacuare Reserve to the Caribbean, and then return us to the dock to begin Section 1-B. We can leave extra equipment at Casa Yolanda in the interim.

Colorful wooden homes line the streets of Cimarrones

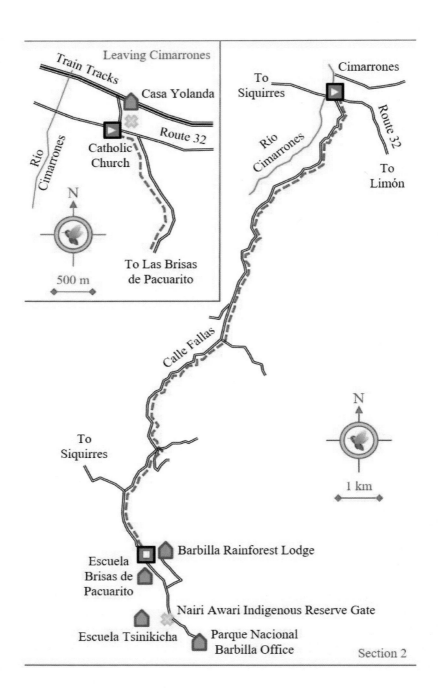

Leaving Cimarrones

Train Tracks

Casa Yolanda

To Siquirres

Cimarrones

Route 32

Catholic Church

Río Cimarrones

Río Cimarrones

Route 32

To Limón

N

500 m

To Las Brisas de Pacuarito

Calle Fallas

To Siquirres

N

1 km

Barbilla Rainforest Lodge

Escuela Brisas de Pacuarito

Nairi Awari Indigenous Reserve Gate

Escuela Tsinikicha

Parque Nacional Barbilla Office

Section 2

Section 2: Cimaronnes – Las Brisas de Pacuarito

Farms dot the hills that rise west of the coastal plains

In this section, we leave the plains and plantations near the coast of the Caribbean and enter rolling hills. Barbed wire fences divide the territory into fields and grazing land, interrupted by stretches of untouched jungle. The trail provides a pathway through the farmland here, and brings us to the edge of indigenous territory. We conclude at the fringe of Parque Nacional Barbilla, with a view of mountains blanketed in the deep green of ancient forests.

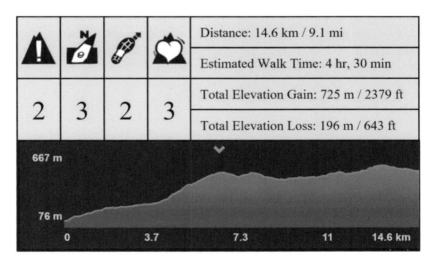

2	3	2	3	Distance: 14.6 km / 9.1 mi
				Estimated Walk Time: 4 hr, 30 min
				Total Elevation Gain: 725 m / 2379 ft
				Total Elevation Loss: 196 m / 643 ft

Cleared hills are used for livestock

Km 0: Cimarrones

This section begins near Iglesia Católica Cimarrones, which sits on the north side of where Route 32 passes the town for which the church is named. The local bus stop offers passengers a connection to Limón or San José. Not even 100 meters east of the church, just up the slope across Route 32, a small shopping area is accessible from the intersection where a gravel road leads further up the same hill. Facing the shops across Route 32, we turn left and cover this short distance. Walking against the direction of traffic increases safety. When traffic is clear, we cross Route 32 and begin our ascent on the gravel road, bearing south. We are entering the Cordillera de Talamanca.

While we gain elevation, we remain on the primary gravel road as it passes private homes and small farms. After 200 meters, a 4-way intersection offers paths into the adjacent slopes, but we continue straight. The forest often lines the trail, and provides protection from the sun as the road curves along the terrain. Our ascent is steady for 1.4 kilometers, then becomes less steep where we pass the gated entrance to the Grand View Estates housing area, on our left. A small community emerges from the forest 1.2 kilometers beyond the large gate of this complex. The dispersed houses line both sides of the trial. In 400 meters, a curve to the right provides a glimpse of the terrain we will cover for the next several kilometers. The steeper slopes are hidden by the dense leaves on tall trees. Gentle hills sit relatively cleared of growth to provide pastures for cattle and horses.

Ascending another 500 meters brings us to a small cluster of homes near the end of a short, steep incline. The trail flattens for a moment, then becomes red mud speckled with rocks, many of which are larger than a fist. Ditches carved by erosion snake through the mud, and the trail hugs the edge of the slope. We continue with a steep drop on one side, and a steep climb on the other. After gaining elevation for another kilometer, we can look back at the ground covered between the coast and Cimarrones. Ahead, the trail narrows, and the jungle encroaches.

Altitude provides a view of the Caribbean

We follow a dirt path between dense trees on the right and cleared fields on the left. Only a barbed wire fence separates us from the cattle that graze on the slopes. Various side trails lead into the fields, often blocked by gates constructed of barbed wire and branches. We go straight past them as the road reaches the crest of a ridge. The view to the right presents a sweeping perspective of the mountains, including Turrialba Volcano. Now 6.7 kilometers from Cimarrones, we encounter a Y-intersection where we veer left to keep the elevation we have gained. This path takes us past more farms with barbed wire fences that keep us on the trail.

Another 700 meters brings us to a 4-way intersection where no two options are the same. A gate blocks the road to our left, and the path quickly fades into the jungle to our right. We go straight, up a steep slope on a narrow footpath through tall grass. In a few hundred meters, this path takes us into a thick patch of jungle where the canopy conceals the sky. When we emerge from the trees, fences continue to guide us along the trail. Even at a 4-way intersection 10.2 kilometers from Cimarrones, gates of barbed wire dictate that we turn right and remain on the primary dirt road.

In 200 meters, we pass a farmhouse with outlying buildings on the right, and then enter another section of trail shaded by trees. Wide branches, carefully positioned, form walkways through pockets of deep mud for the next 600 meters. We descend a short, steep slope, and observe another farm to the right. The road climbs and curves to the left for 500 meters, and then brings us to a complex intersection: two trails both head to the right. We take the inside turn, which remains on level terrain, and keep the pasture immediately on our right side. The trail continues curving gently for 1.4 kilometers, first gradually up a slope, then more steeply. Near the end of this ascent, logs reinforce the mud of the trail before the dirt becomes gravel. We arrive at a T-intersection, with a view of forested hills that the indigenous Cabécar tribes occupy.

Isolated homes built from simple materials appear along the trail

At this T-intersection, we turn left onto the main gravel road, and proceed south. The edge of Las Brisas de Pacuarito is 1.3 kilometers down this road. A sign next to a sports field prohibits hunting, and marks the entrance to the community. Escuela Brisas de Pacuarito is 200 meters past this field, on the right side of the road.

The section ends at the payphones outside the school gate, but they may not function. The curriculum here reinforces the environmental message promoted in the area, which supports agrarian culture amid the growing market for eco-tourism. Students represent a mix of the nearby indigenous and mestizo communities. Instruction includes classes in the Cabécar tribal language, to help preserve this culture for future generations. The local office for Parque Nacional Barbilla also encourages preservation and natural sciences, and offers workshops for people from the surrounding villages.

Km 14.6: Las Brisas de Pacuarito

If we continue 800 meters beyond the school, a dirt road to the left leads towards Barbilla Rainforest Lodge. We can also veer right and follow the primary road, which ends at the Parque Nacional Barbilla ranger station. On the way to the station, we descend a section of pavement for 400 meters. From the base of this slope, we cover another kilometer of gravel to the park office. The rangers can provide information about the forest, but do not allow hikers to sleep on the grounds. Camping here is not permitted, and no food or resources are available. The ranger station is not affiliated with El Camino de Costa Rica.

Escuela Tsinikicha is only accessible with a guide from the local tribe

Another lodging option near Las Brisas de Pacuarito is inside the Nairi Awari Indigenous Reserve, which borders Parque Nacional Barbilla. Entrance to this territory is controlled by the Cabécar people. A local guide is required here, and should be arranged in advance. If guided into the territory, campers can sleep on a covered platform inside the grounds of Escuela Tsinikicha, the tribal school. To find the school, or rendezvous with a guide at the entrance to the territory, we continue 300 meters from the bottom of the paved downhill section on the way to the ranger station. Rather than continue to the park office, we stop at a gate in the fence with a sign for the school. Both are on the right, where a clearing dips down to a creek. The school is approximately 500 meters past this entrance to the tribal territory, on the other side of a patch of trees that conceals another creek. Guides will take people to the school for camping, but return to their families in the evening to allow for privacy. If arranged early, campers can access the school kitchen, but must provide their own food.

To Cimarrones

Escuela Brisas de Pacuarito

Gate

Escuela Tsinikicha

Río Dantas

N

500 m

Nocle

Tsiobata

Section 3

Section 3: Las Brisas de Pacuarito – Tsiobata

The jungle trail is often just a narrow dirt or mud path

Once we depart the village of Las Brisas de Pacuarito, we will not encounter a store until the far side of the tribal land. Knowing the upcoming distance and remoteness, we can plan ahead and purchase any necessities before we leave the village. Small shops carry non-perishable food that will add little weight to a pack, but provide valuable energy as we cross the jungle. The jungle itself is wild.

⚠️	🧭	👣	❤️	Distance: 12.5 km / 7.8 mi
				Estimated Walk Time: 7 hr, 50 min
4	4	4	3	Total Elevation Gain: 550 m / 1804 ft
				Total Elevation Loss: 664 m / 2178 ft

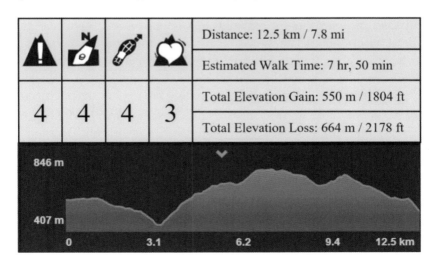

Km 0: Las Brisas de Pacuarito

This section begins at Escuela Brisas de Pacuarito. Exiting the school, we turn right on a gravel road and follow it to the south. After 800 meters, a dirt side road leads back to the left, but we stay on the gravel as it climbs over a small hill to the right. On the far side of this hill, pavement helps vehicles maintain traction.

As we descend, the sports field used by residents of the tribal village comes into view. At the bottom of the pavement, we see scattered homes constructed from dried palm leaves in the traditional style. Some of these buildings are adjacent to modern wooden houses. The farms on the right side of the road are inside the Nairi Awari Indigenous Reserve, which shares its southern border with Parque Nacional Barbilla. The entrance to the Reserve is 300 meters past the end of the pavement. The gate is marked by a sign for Escuela Tsinikicha on the right.

Km 1.8: Nairi Awari Indigenous Reserve

A match on the field in the Nairi Awari Indigenous Reserve

We stop at the sign for the tribal school, and turn right to face a barbed wire fence gate. Without a local guide, we cannot pass the gate: entering the tribal territory unaccompanied is prohibited, and disrespectful of the local Cabécar culture. There are several places along the gravel road where we can rendezvous with a guide, so long as coordination is conducted in advance. We can use Escuela Brisas de Pacuarito, or the gate at the territory entrance, or the office of Parque Nacional Barbilla, which is 700 meters farther down the gravel road. Without a prearranged guide, the park office is the safest place to acquire assistance with the process of hiring one.

With our local guide, we can pass through the barbed wire gate and continue downhill on a narrow foot path. Wooden planks serve as bridges across creeks as we continue straight towards the jungle. In 300 meters we enter the trees and cross another, sturdier bridge over a shaded creek. Just past this creek, we veer right through a gap in a fence, and bypass the grounds of Escuela Tsinikicha. Our guide can also escort us onto the school yard, where lodging is available if arranged in advance.

Escuela Tsinikicha includes a covered deck, small classrooms, a traditional palm leaf building, a shower, and a kitchen. The school also has outlets we can use to charge electronic devices. However, depending on the time of year and day of the week, there may be teachers and students present. Sleeping on the porch next to the main building also leaves us observable to passing villagers, but keeps us protected from rain.

The narrow path that leads across the creeks to Escuela Tsinikicha

Beyond the gap in the fence outside Escuela Tsinikicha, we use a footpath that keeps the school on our left and guides us down a gentle slope for 300 meters. This brings us to the edge of the jungle. From here, our local guide is the surest way to safely navigate the hazards of the wilderness and emerge on the far side of the indigenous territory at the proper place. Among the trees, there are narrow, shifting, unmarked trails that crisscross and loop back on El Camino de Costa Rica. The damp red clay creates a risk of injury from slipping or tripping over exposed roots. Rivers must be crossed, and can be swift, with water up to the waist. Forest maintenance efforts, farming, and erosion can erase previous routes and create new ones. The thick foliage also blocks reception on mobile devices. Fortunately, a local guide can assist with contacting emergency services via community resources, which would be unavailable to independent travelers. And a guide from the tribe is not only recommended as a precaution, and as a show of respect for the local people: it is required by law. We do not proceed without one.

We enter the jungle, and continue to descend terrain with varying degrees of steepness for one kilometer, until we arrive at Río Mono. There is no bridge across this river, but it can be crossed on foot. Depending on the season, the water can be one meter deep, and swift. Stairs on the far side of the river lead uphill to the right.

An intersection 500 meters beyond the crossing presents two trails, and we take the narrow option on the right side, up another incline. Our climb continues for 3.6 kilometers on a trail that sometimes consists of slick mud. Some sections are less steep than others, but as we walk along a rising ridge, we gain more than 300 meters in elevation. Several paths and trails cross El Camino de Costa Rica along this stretch of the jungle. Some are wider than ours, and in better condition, which makes them more appealing and therefore dangerous. But as we ascend through the trees, our guide ensures we avoid diversions that lead us away from the correct route.

The trail through the jungle

The trail becomes level, then gradually descends for 1.5 kilometers. More paths intersect our own, but often turn back to areas we have already passed. At the end of this descent, we begin to climb out of a small valley, and cross the first in a series of streams. The stream crossings conclude within one kilometer, and the ascent ends shortly thereafter. Just over the hill, we find an intersection with a wide path to the left, and a narrow path that continues straight. The wide path leads to Valle Escondido, much further southeast. We take the narrow, less-developed route, which may require a short detour through the brush. On this trail, our guide leads us forward for just over a kilometer. We ignore the narrow side trails during this gentle descent.

Km 11.0: Nocle

At the entrance to a tribal community in the depths of the jungle

The canopy opens overhead, and we arrive at a rustic gate. This marks the entrance to the tribal community of Noclé. In farming communities like this one, a local guide enables us to walk confidently past indigenous homes and around private gardens. We remain close to the tree line, skirting the right edge of the village. A barbed wire fence greets us after 200 meters. We pass through the gate and proceed for another 600 meters under the canopy to a Y-intersection. Veering left, we come to a left turn, and avoid the small trails that lead to homes and farms.

Our route continues straight down a slope, across a stream, to another gate in a barbed wire fence. Passing through this gate brings us into the community of Tsiobata. Two nearby buildings, constructed in the traditional style, serve as a cultural preservation space for the Cabécar people that dwell in the Nairi Awari land. These structures, called Casas Cosmogonicas, contain information and objects on display that can teach us about the local people and communities.

Km 12.5: Tsiobata

The homes in Tsiobata hide among the trees. Few are visible from the trail as we travel with our guide along a footpath through the central clearing. Cattle graze freely here, and we remain mindful to provide them with sufficient distance and not provoke them. With prior coordination and help from our guide, we can stay overnight at Escuela Tsiobata and have meals prepared from local ingredients. The section ends here, but we may choose to continue with the next and exit the jungle.

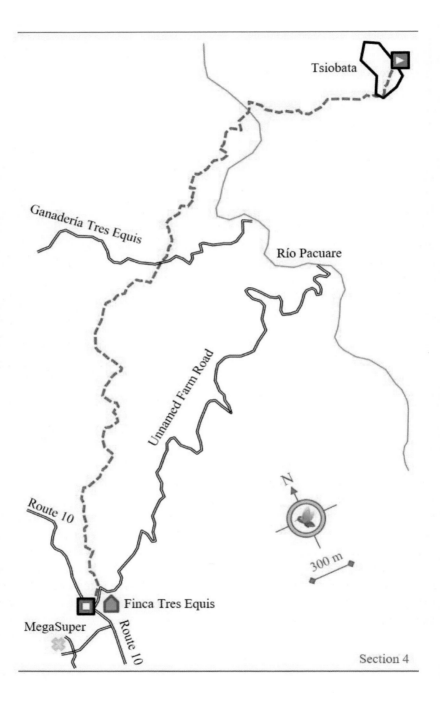

Tsiobata

Ganadería Tres Equis

Río Pacuare

Unnamed Farm Road

N

300 m

Route 10

Finca Tres Equis

MegaSuper

Route 10

Section 4

Section 4: Tsiobata – Tres Equis

Sunrise seen over the Nairi Awari Indigenous Reserve

This section begins inside the Cabécar tribal territory, where few resources are available. For this reason, coordination with a local guide to combine Section 3 and Section 4 is suggested. Otherwise, we wake in the indigenous community and prepare to descend to Río Pacuare. On the far side of the river valley, horse and cattle ranches are a common site. We pass many of them on the way to the town of Tres Equis. Supplies and lodging can be acquired once we reach this community.

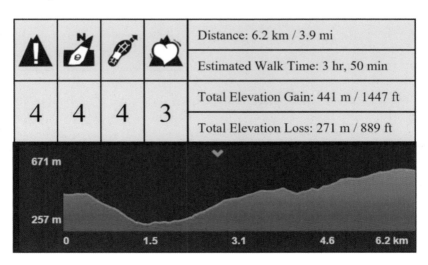

4	4	4	3	Distance: 6.2 km / 3.9 mi
				Estimated Walk Time: 3 hr, 50 min
				Total Elevation Gain: 441 m / 1447 ft
				Total Elevation Loss: 271 m / 889 ft

Km 0: Tsiobata

A traditional home built next to a modern home is common in the Reserve

The central clearing of Tsiobata stretches for 300 meters. Our route through it runs alongside a stream to our right. We cross this stream to enter the jungle, and begin our descent to Río Pacuare. The trail slopes downhill for 1.2 kilometers, with switchbacks and the possibility of crossing small, seasonal streams along the way. At the base of the descent, we arrive at the east bank of the river. To access the bridge, we climb onto a metal platform anchored to the terrain a safe distance from the waterline.

Km 1.5: Río Pacuare

The "bridge" across Río Pacuare consists of a metal basket that slides along a cable, and a rope that loops around pulleys on both sides of the river. Platforms allow passengers to climb into the basket while it is secured with a hook. Passengers pull themselves across using the rope, which is tied to the basket and creates a conveyer system. A local guide can assist with pulling from the riverbank. With two or more people, crossing is easier because one person can sit in the basket while others help pull the rope. We must use care when handling the rope system to minimize blisters, and to avoid get pinched by the pulleys. We also want to keep our equipment out of the river, so we secure everything together before leaving the platform. Once across, we leave the basket unhooked so that it can be retrieved from either side of the river.

The crossing at Río Pacuare

On the far side of Río Pacuare, we climb up from the river valley on the steep path to the left. After 700 meters, we encounter a barbed wire fence gate, and the incline increases. A similar gate crosses the path 500 meters later. At the top of this hill, 200 meters past the second gate, we arrive at a T-intersection in a gravel road. Visible to the left, the road becomes paved and descends a different slope down to a point on the river used by rafters to enter the water. We turn right, onto Ganadería Tres Equis, but we only follow this gravel road for 100 meters. Just around a curve, we face another intersection, at the base of a grassy hill. Here the gravel road continues to the right, but our path turns left and cuts up through the pasture. Following the tracks through the grass with our eyes, we can survey the slope, and see where El Camino de Costa Rica reaches a fence line and turns right.

We leave Ganadería Tres Equis, first turning left into the field, then curving right after 100 meters. The fence seen from the road guides us around a ridge for 300 meters to a barbed wire fence gate. Past the gate, the trail makes a deceptive split over a small rise, but we remain on the worn tracks and reconnect with the fence moments later. Another gate crosses the trail in 200 meters, and beyond it we pass a pond on our right, and a small metal shade structure on our left.

Rolling hills provide sustenance for livestock

As the terrain curves to the left for 300 meters, the elevation gives us a view of the mountain ranges that form part of Parque Nacional Barbilla and the adjacent tribal lands. We pass through another gate, and follow level ground for 400 meters. A curve to the right and a quick descent into a patch of trees brings us to a creek. We cross, and ascend for 100 meters on the far side of this water source. After we pass through another gate, we take a hard right turn. The quality and visibility of the trail diminishes from here. Sometimes we follow a path as thin as a single tire tread and as faint as an animal trail through the tall grass.

Attuned to the details of the trail, we continue 200 meters beyond the gate and curve right along the crest of a small ridge. Panoramic views to the left must not prevent us from using good judgement and patience when analyzing the way forward, as we arc up a hill to the left after 100 meters. In front of us, the road gains definition as it passes between two embankments for 100 meters, then fades and turns right along a path through a small saddle in the ridge ahead. Over the ridge, we cover another 100 meters to find a gate on the close side of a creek. We pass through the gate, cross the creek, and enter a field of thick grass and bushes.

The trail follows rustic fences that delineate large ranches

The footpath takes us 100 meters through this field, then uphill on a wider path. Up this incline 100 meters, we veer right through more gates. The path here is wide enough to accommodate a vehicle as it follows the curve of the terrain. At a Y-intersection in another 100 meters, we veer left to maintain our elevation, and can soon hear sounds of traffic from the freeway that runs through Tres Equis. Beyond the Y-intersection, 200 more meters, we avoid the steep road up the hill to the left, and veer right on level ground. This leads us 300 meters through orchid fields to a barbed wire fence gate.

Through this gate, we approach Finca Tres Equis, a coffee and cacao farm. The painted wooden fence lining the trail guides us onto a maintained gravel road that connects the farm home with the main gate. We enter the farm on this gravel road, and veer right towards the cabins where guests can stay. There is also space for camping, and opportunities to tour the farm and sample products, if coordinated in advance. Beyond the cabins, we exit the gate and step onto Route 10. The section ends here.

Km 6.2: Tres Equis

The private road through Finca Tres Equis leads down to Río Pacuare

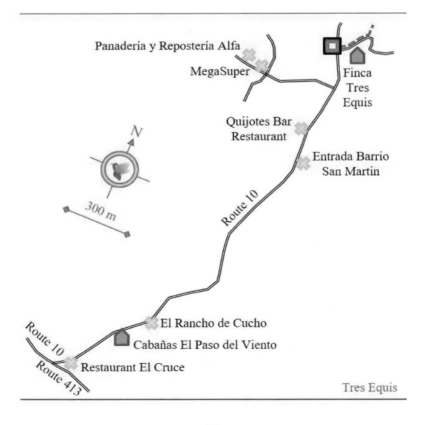

Panadería y Repostería Alfa

MegaSuper

Finca Tres Equis

Quijotes Bar Restaurant

Entrada Barrio San Martin

N

300 m

Route 10

El Rancho de Cucho

Route 10

Cabañas El Paso del Viento

Route 413

Restaurant El Cruce

Tres Equis

To purchase food and supplies in Tres Equis, we exit the gate of Finca Tres Equis and turn left onto Route 10. For safety, we walk facing traffic and use the sidewalk to cover 200 meters. Looking right, we see a road leading down a slope into the town, with a view of Turrialba Volcano in the distance. This road takes us past the sports field and a cemetery to the main town intersection, 300 meters from Route 10. On our right we see the MegaSuper market, which offers a variety of food and hygiene times. If we continue along the main road for another 100 meters past this store, we find Panaderia y Reposteria Alfa on the right, selling fresh baked goods.

Route 10 also leads to several restaurants, if we continue south from Finca Tres Equis. Quijotes Bar Restaurant is the closest, 400 meters from the farm gate. Another restaurant, Entrada Barrio San Martin, is 100 meters farther south. El Rancho de Cucho is 1.7 kilometers south of the gate, and Restaurant El Cruce is 2.1 kilometers to the south. Between El Rancho de Cucho and Restaurant El Cruce we can find lodging at Cabañas El Paso del Viento, but the main attraction at this destination is the chocolate made from beans grown locally.

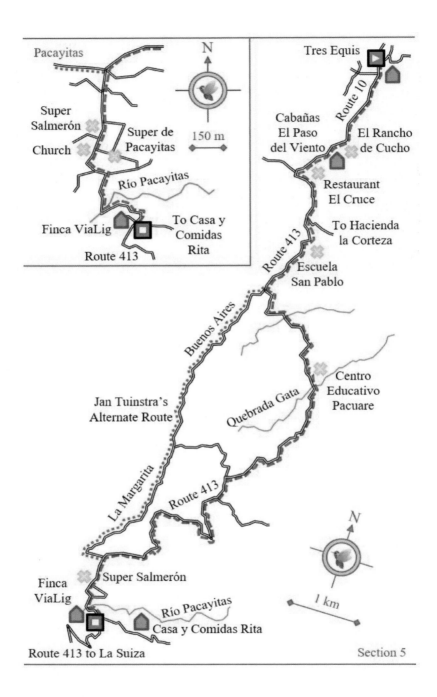

Pacayitas

N

Super
Salmerón
Church

Super de
Pacayitas

150 m

Río Pacayitas

Finca ViaLig

To Casa y
Comidas
Rita

Route 413

Tres Equis

Route 10

Cabañas
El Paso
del Viento

El Rancho
de Cucho

Restaurant
El Cruce

Route 413

To Hacienda
la Corteza

Escuela
San Pablo

Buenos Aires

Centro
Educativo
Pacuare

Jan Tuinstra's
Alternate Route

Quebrada Gata

La Margarita

Route 413

N

1 km

Finca
ViaLig

Super Salmerón

Río Pacayitas

Casa y Comidas Rita

Route 413 to La Suiza

Section 5

70

Section 5: Tres Equis – Pacayitas

Turrialba Volcano seen from Finca Tres Equis

The trail here traverses ranches and fields crowded with dense, tall sugarcane. Villages along the way introduce us to the quality of life in rural Costa Rica. Each community we pass has its small shops, schools, and churches, along with farms offering tours and samples of produce from the local area.

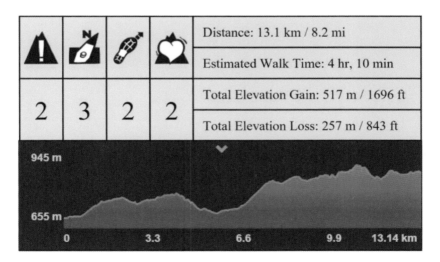

⚠ 2	🧭 3	👢 2	❤ 2	Distance: 13.1 km / 8.2 mi
				Estimated Walk Time: 4 hr, 10 min
				Total Elevation Gain: 517 m / 1696 ft
				Total Elevation Loss: 257 m / 843 ft

Km 0: Tres Equis

Outside the tall gates of Finca Tres Equis, we step onto National Primary Route 10 and turn left to travel south. We use the sidewalk for safety, and walk facing traffic. After 200 meters, a side street on our right leads into the town of Tres Equis, but we continue straight between bus stops on both sides of the main road. Looking to the right, we have a view of the eastern slopes of Turrialba Volcano, the top of which may be hidden in the clouds.

Route 10 leads us past several restaurants, the first of which is Quijotes Bar Restaurant, 400 meters from the Finca Tres Equis gate. El Rancho de Cucho, designed to look like a log cabin, is 1.3 kilometers south of Quijotes Bar Restaurant, followed closely by Cabañas El Paso del Viento. This establishment offers specialty chocolates made from beans grown on the nearby slopes. A few hundred meters farther along, we arrive at Restaurant El Cruce, which has two levels and a covered outdoor dining area. This location dominates the intersection of Route 10 and Route 413. The two roads join near a sign reading "Pacayitas 10 km." Other signs point to Trapiche, San Vincente, and Mollejones. We will see similar signs as we follow Route 413, which slopes downhill to the left, behind Restaurant El Cruce.

The arrows on local village signs do not always match the direction of the trail

Route 413 continues as intermittent gravel and broken pavement for 800 meters before reaching a Y-intersection where a sign points right to Mollejones. The other road leads to Hacienda la Corteza, a large ranch that grazes its stock in the pastures on our left. We veer right, up a slope, and approach the village of San Pablo. After

300 meters we veer right again, past land belonging to Finca Orgánica Cañaveral, towards the school visible up the hill. This school, with its vibrant floral garden, sits on the left side of the road, with a small shop across the street. Past the school and market, we stay straight on Route 413 for 600 meters and arrive at the San Pablo community church. At a Y-intersection 400 meters beyond the church, we follow the sign for Trapiche and veer left. A sign for Mollejones points to the right, but this time we ignore it. Due to the steepness of Route 413 in this area, the road becomes paved 300 meters past this intersection.

The garden at Escuela San Pablo

After descending 400 meters, the pavement ends at a concrete slab bridge amid horse ranches and small farms. A tiny shrine stands just past this bridge, on our left. The stream here is one of two waterways in this valley. We transit the valley on a gravel road, except in places where the incline is particularly steep. After 1.2 kilometers, we arrive at the village of Pacuare.

Km 6.2: Pacuare

In Pacuare, we proceed with the Catholic church on our right, and the Centro Educativo Pacuare on our left. In 100 meters, we cross Quebrada Gata. This deep, narrow river is the second water source we encounter that flows through this valley into Río Pacuare. Just past the river, a sign for Trapiche points to the left, but this time we ignore it. We veer right and begin an ascent that becomes steeper as we continue.

This incline up Route 413 concludes after 1.3 kilometers. We continue along the main road another 600 meters, and stay straight on the gravel when a side road intersects our path from the right. In 400 meters, at a curved T-intersection marked by a yellow cross, we turn left onto a downhill slope and follow a roadside fence. This leads into fields of sugarcane, which we navigate for 400 meters. At a T-intersection where a bus stop sits on our right, we ignore the sign that points to Mollejones. Instead, we turn right around the bus stop, towards Corredores Del Pacuare.

From the bus stop near the sign pointing to Corredores Del Pacuare, we ascend for 800 meters to a sweeping right turn that provides a broad view of the valley on our left. A blue well enclosed in a cage marks the top of this particular climb. In 300 meters, we veer right and begin another gradual ascent, this time leading to the highest elevation on this section. After 900 meters, we start our descent and pass homes on the outskirts of Pacayitas. The road continues in varying conditions until it rounds a left turn after 1.2 kilometers and points directly into town.

The valley created by Río Pacayitas, and the community named after the river

Around this corner, we continue straight past a side road that meets ours from the right. Ahead of us, we see a sign proclaiming Bienvenidos a Pacayitas next to a concrete bridge. We pass the sign, and arrive in the town center after 200 meters. Liceo Rural Pacayitas is on our right, and the central plaza is on our left. As we proceed, we pass Super Salmeron and continue up a hill past the church on our right. The road twists up this hill, and we stay on the pavement. In 500 meters, we cross a concrete slab over a gulley. The final 300 meters of this section takes us around a corner to the right, where we stop at the entrance to Finca ViaLig. Signs nearby mark one of the key intersections in the community.

Km 13.2: Pacayitas

Finca ViaLig offers lodging, homestays, and camping sites, depending on our desired level of amenities. The company also provides tours in the local area, and can customize experiences that include hiking the entire length of El Camino de Costa Rica. A restaurant on site offers breakfast, lunch, and dinner. Another lodging and dining option in Pacayitas is Casa y Comidas Rita, located 700 meters to the left, down the gravel road that intersects the pavement in front of Finca ViaLig. At Casa y Comidas Rita, guests stay in the multi-room lodge across the street from the restaurant. Wi-fi is available in the dining area, which is adjacent to the family home.

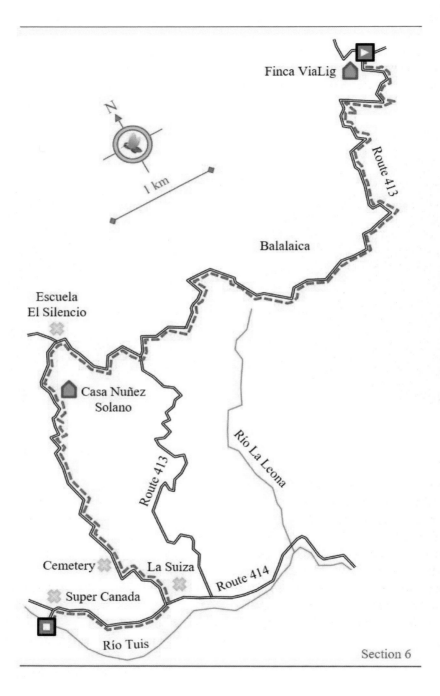

Finca ViaLig

Route 413

Balalaica

Escuela
El Silencio

Casa Nuñez
Solano

Río La Leona

Route 413

Cemetery

La Suiza

Route 414

Super Canada

Río Tuis

Section 6

Section 6: Pacayitas – La Suiza

Storm clouds gather over Lake Angostura

The first portion of this section passes through rolling hills blanketed with pastures that begin at the summit of the road leading up from Pacayitas. After descending from these hills, the trail continues through villages on the outskirts of La Suiza. This city is one of the largest on the trail, with several convenient shops and businesses to facilitate recovery, resupply, and preparation for the next few sections.

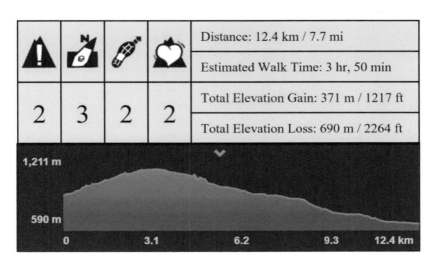

⚠️	🧭	👣	❤️	Distance: 12.4 km / 7.7 mi
				Estimated Walk Time: 3 hr, 50 min
2	3	2	2	Total Elevation Gain: 371 m / 1217 ft
				Total Elevation Loss: 690 m / 2264 ft

Km 0: Pacayitas

This section begins on Route 413, at the entrance to Finca ViaLig. Starting with the Finca ViaLig sign on our right, we walk straight along this paved road towards a mountainside covered with sugarcane. Going forward 100 meters, the road first curves left and then climbs using several switchbacks. The pavement is often in poor condition, and can be quite crowded when two vehicles pass each other. The tall sugarcane also makes seeing around turns difficult, so we pay attention to traffic from both directions. When we reach the top of the hill and look back to the right, we have a view of Pacayitas and the valley it occupies. The region ahead of us is Balalaica, with land conducive to ranching and farming. Around the corner, gates bearing names like Rancho Finca Balalaica, on the left, give homage to the history and culture of the area. The pavement transitions to gravel after 1.8 kilometers, and the steep climb ends.

Looking back at Pacayitas after reaching the hilltop on Route 413

The gravel continues, with patches of asphalt on steeper sections. We curve for 1.5 kilometers along the side of a slope that drops off to the left, where dense trees and close ridgelines block the view. Suddenly we reenter sugarcane fields, and then emerge on a broad plateau. To the left, across sweeping pastures, green ridges fade into the horizon. Distant white specks become cattle upon closer inspection. An occasional farm house, with a roof of corrugated metal, peeks between the trees. We follow along the barbed wire fence that lines the wide road until we reenter thick, high sugarcane, and are no longer able to see the distant hills.

The trail begins its long descent to La Suiza. At a tight turn to the right, on a steeper incline, the sugarcane on our left parts for a moment and we can see Lake Angostura and the towns surrounding it. Farther down this ridge, we arrive at a Y-intersection with a bus stop and a sign announcing Coope Pueblos Unidos. We turn right towards the sign. After 1.2 kilometers, we find the school in El Silencio on our right, across from the village sports field, with an adjacent market and a decorated bus stop nearby. At this intersection, we turn left, and proceed with the field now on our right as the descent continues.

A ranch in the fields of Balalaica

After 500 meters on this gravel road, we round a curve and encounter a small clearing on our right, with a pedestrian gate that allows entry between a row of bushes. This family garden includes a variety of fruit trees, beyond which a plot of sugarcane covers the downhill slope. The view across the garden includes Lake Angostura, Turrialba Volcano, and the city of Turrialba, which stretches up the mountain from the valley floor. On our left, a concrete slab helps ascend the driveway to Casa Nuñez Solano. The garden and sugarcane belongs to this family. They provide homestays and meals, and allow camping under the trees on their land.

A few hundred meters past the Casa Nuñez Solano garden viewpoint, the road descends more steeply. Pavement provides traction for vehicles on the severe grades. At a junction where two roads curve to the right, we take the farther one in a wide turn past the village of El Carmen. Following the gravel for 500 meters leads us to a double-decker cabin adorned with crafts and paintings belonging to Familia Fonseca Gomez, according to the sign hanging from the porch. Another kilometer takes us to a cemetery that lines the right side of the road on the outskirts of La Suiza. From here, the road is paved until near the end of this section.

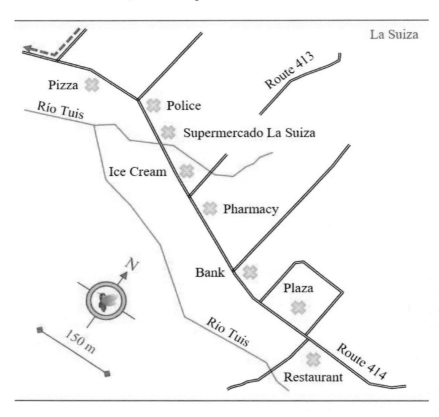

On the right, we spot a sign for Barrio Linda Vista, and then pass a row of colorful houses on our left. At the end of this street is a sign for Barrio Santa Rita de Casia. Here the trail forms a T-intersection with Route 414 in La Suiza. The center of town, with shops and other resources, is to the left, across a small bridge. El Camino de Costa Rica continues to the right for another kilometer.

Km 11.4: La Suiza

As we turn away from La Suiza on Route 414, the final kilometer of this section immediately passes the large Colegio Tecnico Profesional La Suiza-Turrialba. We then enter the adjacent community of Canadá. The indicators of this transition include Super Canada, a market on our right, and Carniceria Canada, a shop on our left. When we arrive at the intersection with these two businesses and a bus stop, we turn left. Down a short dirt road, we reach the bridge over Río Tuis, where the section ends.

La Suiza: If we turn left instead of right on Route 414 and cross the small bridge that leads to the center of La Suiza, we can find several resources within a few hundred meters. Remaining on Route 414, the first restaurant available is Cirilo's Pizza, on the right. Past the first side street, we see the police station, and then Supermercado La Suiza. Bright block letters spell out the name of the city on the opposite side of the street. Beyond the next side street is a Panaderia y Reposteria, Kenneth's Ice Cream, and a pharmacy. After additional restaurants and markets, 500 meters from the bridge near the pizza place, we find a Banco Nacional with an ATM. The large city plaza is past the bank, but this is far enough if all we require are supplies and more of the local currency. From here, we can turn back to the west and reconnect with El Camino de Costa Rica on the way out of town.

Km 12.4: Río Tuis

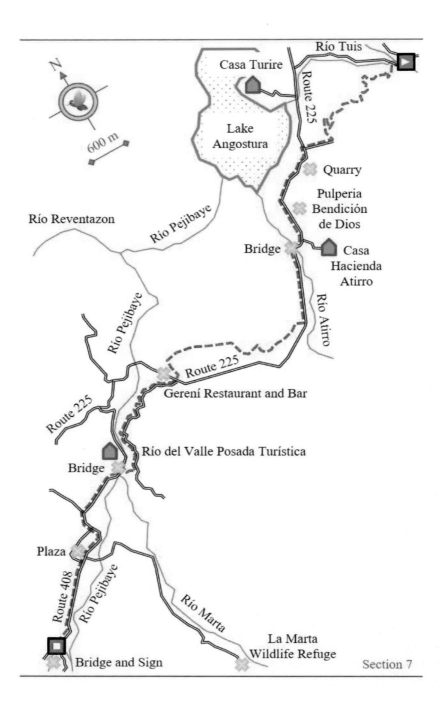

Casa Turire

Río Tuis

Route 225

Lake
Angostura

Quarry

Pulperia
Bendición
de Dios

Río Reventazon

Río Pejibaye

Bridge

Casa
Hacienda
Atirro

Río Atirro

Río Pejibaye

Route 225

Route 225

Gereni Restaurant and Bar

Río del Valle Posada Turística

Bridge

Plaza

Route 408

Río Pejibaye

Río Marta

La Marta
Wildlife Refuge

Bridge and Sign

Section 7

N

600 m

Section 7: La Suiza – Humo de Pejibaye

Mountains seen from the path through fields near La Suiza

This section includes two of the more prominent cities on the trail: La Suiza and Pejibaye. There are bridges to cross, rivers to follow, farmland and plantations to navigate, and a shaded path through the woods to enjoy. With ample opportunities to pause for refreshments, this section allows us to prepare for the remote areas that follow, when large communities are not conveniently located directly on the route.

!	⊕	🍾	♥	Distance: 16.3 km / 10.1 mi
				Estimated Walk Time: 5 hr
2	3	2	3	Total Elevation Gain: 476 m / 1562 ft
				Total Elevation Loss: 373 m / 1224 ft

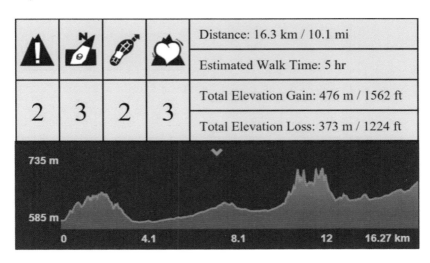

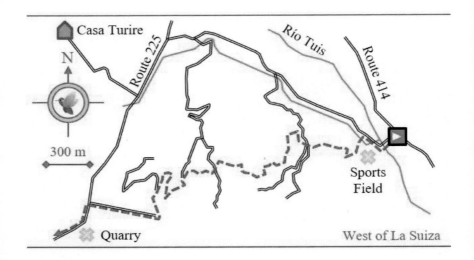

Km 0: La Suiza

We leave La Suiza through the neighborhood of Canadá, starting near Super Canada and Carniceria Canada. These shops are on opposite corners of an intersection along Route 414, where a dirt side road leads 100 meters to the bridges over Río Tuis. The metal pedestrian bridge is to the left of the larger vehicle bridge, so we take the smaller one to be safe. As we cross, our motion causes the bridge to bounce, but the support wires remain secure. On the opposite side of the footbridge, we turn right and walk past the vehicle bridge towards a sports field. After 200 meters, beyond a concrete slab bridge, the field is on our left. We circle around it onto a narrow dirt road that leads uphill, rather than continue into the farmland directly ahead of us. Our path takes us into terrain dedicated to growing coffee and sugarcane.

A couple hundred meters up the hill, the trail makes a hairpin turn to the right and continues to ascend. On a straight stretch, we pass a gated farm entrance and arrive at a multi-directional intersection. Some trails lead up, and others lead down, but we forge straight ahead between two wooden posts, on level ground. The next 200 meters brings us to a pair of paths that turn left, and we follow the inside curve up an incline.

At the top of the hill ahead of us on the left, we observe a small shade structure for workers harvesting sugarcane, but this is not along our route. Our shade comes from the thick sugarcane and reeds growing on our left as we walk a grassy trail with views of the distant volcanos to the north: Irazú on the left, and Turrialba on the right. Leaving the high reeds and groups of tall trees, we reach an X-intersection. One trail comes up the slope behind us from the right to connect with ours, and two others split across the terrain in front of us. We push forward to the right, on a slight incline up and around the hill on our right side. After 200 meters, we descend past a view of Lake Angostura with mountains in the background. A solitary tree at the bottom of this slope offers us a spot to pause and take a picture of the scenery from the comfort of its shade.

Lake Angostura shines on a sunny day, but clouds conceal the mountaintops

Continuing through the fields, we curve first to the left, then down and around the slope of the terrain in front of us as it veers to the right. Across the next 400 meters, we encounter a hairpin turn to the right, and then a wider left turn around a pocket of coffee plants. From there, the path leads us off the hills to a pair of low metal pillars that mark the exit of the plantation. The cable between the pillars is easy to avoid.

Beyond the pillars, we turn right and proceed directly to the paved road visible through 500 meters of sugarcane: Route 225. To our left we will enter the town of Atirro, along El Camino de Costa Rica, but there is lodging available just under two kilometers to the right, at Casa Turire. The 900 meters to the front gate leaves another 800 meters to the hotel itself, but the hotel and restaurant are among the most sumptuous to be found along the entire trail.

Turning left onto Route 225, we follow the guard rail around a curve to the right, past a quarry. Beyond the quarry, the bold sign for Lam's Snacks does not mean food is available here. The company manufactures snack foods using crops harvested locally. Rancho Palma also does not offer food or lodging. Instead, it serves the community as a place for events like weddings. Our next opportunity to purchase supplies is around the next curve to the left, at Pulperia Bendición de Dios. Palms line the following stretch of road, which leads to the local church and school. Just outside the church we find a colorful sign for Atirro, confirming which town we have entered.

Sugarcane fields fill the wide valleys in this region

Km 4.8: Atirro

Just past the church, Route 225 veers right, near the Agroatirro R. L. sugarcane processing plant. The gravel road that runs to the left of the plant leads 600 meters up a hill to Casa Hacienda Atirro, which offers lodging with a garden that guests can explore to pick fruit. By staying on the pavement and following the trail, we cross Río Atirro on the same bridge that vehicles use. On the far side of the bridge, the road bends left and continues with sugarcane fields on both sides.

We travel straight for 1.3 kilometers on the main paved road through these fields before turning right onto a dirt access road that leads into the sugarcane. The access road guides us to the base of the ridge now in front of us, where we turn left. The trail then follows the curve of the terrain around to the right. The path in this area is often clogged with tall grass, and meant for farm vehicles and high-clearance trucks that transport crops. As we proceed, we may spot shelters for farmers with motorbikes parked nearby, or see their wagons loaded with harvested sugarcane.

Once we are around the ridge and facing north, we turn left at a T-intersection onto a more maintained dirt road through the fields, and remain on level ground rather than pursue the slope into the hills. After 200 meters, a right turn at a T-intersection takes us down a smooth gravel road, which leads toward two rows of pine trees. We look straight down the path between the rows of trees: this is the way.

Beyond the pines, we ignore any slanted intersecting crossroads while traveling straight ahead for 800 meters. Then the gravel path curves left, just in front of a home tucked in the trees. After a turn to the right, we cover the last 100 meters and reconnect with Route 225. On our right is the Gerení Restaurant and Bar, and to our left we can look down Route 225 where it skirts the fields we just navigated.

We do not follow Route 225. Instead, we take the gravel road just across the street, which continues into forested hills. This road follows curves in the terrain that veer right, along an embankment. The first kilometer ascends. At the high point, we remain close to the same altitude for 800 meters, and then descend towards a collection of homes on the right side of the road.

Halfway down this slope, we look between the buildings on our right and see a narrow path between them. Taking this path, we walk between two barbed wire fences to a view of the footbridge over Río Pejibaye. The small bridge sways under us as we cross over the river. On the far side, we turn left around the bus stop and head south on Route 408. Sometimes called Calle Pejibaye, this paved road leads directly to the center of the town that shares its name. For lodging and meals outside of Pejibaye, we can turn right instead, and proceed 200 meters north on Route 408, to Río del Valle Posada Turística.

A path through the pine trees

Following Route 408 to the left, after crossing the footbridge over the river, we cover a kilometer through the outskirts of Pejibaye. At a Y-intersection, we veer left, and then continue straight where a side road intersects the main road from the right. A sign pointing to La Marta indicates the presence of a local wildlife refuge, although this establishment is not on El Camino de Costa Rica. Our road curves to the right, and leads directly to the town plaza.

Looking back from Route 408 across the bridge over Río Pejibaye

Km 14.4: Pejibaye

The trail passes by the plaza, which remains on our right as we follow a pedestrian walkway along a row of buildings. At the next intersection, Supermercado Maraya and Super La Leyenda both sell food and supplies. There are also small cafés, restaurants, and a towering church with a long flight of stairs near this crossing. We continue straight, and soon find the local school. The road here has a sidewalk, which we use. A yellow line tracks down the middle of the pavement to help us hold our course. We pass housing areas, and have occasional views of the river on our left. After a kilometer, we have crossed a yellow footbridge to the left of a concrete slab bridge for vehicles and arrived at a welcoming sign: Bienvenidos a El Humo.

Km 16.3: Humo de Pejibaye

Río Pejibaye, seen from the bridge, looking south

On the way through Humo de Pejibaye, often referred to simply as Humo, we pass Super Evelyn #2. This is the final large market before we enter and pass over the mountains on the approach to Parque Nacional Tapantí. After 400 meters, we reach the center of town, using the footbridge to the right of a vehicle bridge. Another sign greets us, and indicates that Refugio de Vida Silvestre El Copal is to the left. This is our path, but the sign marks the end of this section. A paved road leads uphill to the right, but we have already passed sufficient opportunities to purchase supplies and have no need to proceed further into Humo.

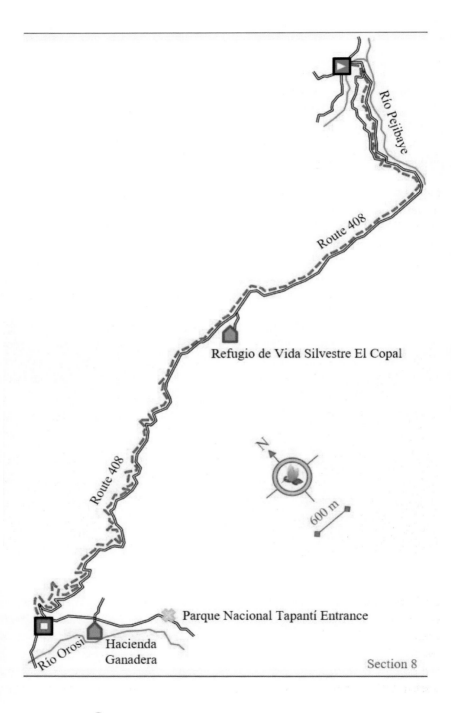

Río Pejibaye

Route 408

Refugio de Vida Silvestre El Copal

N

600 m

Route 408

Parque Nacional Tapantí Entrance

Río Orosi

Hacienda
Ganadera

Section 8

Section 8: Humo de Pejibaye – Tapantí

The sign outside nearby Parque Nacional Tapantí

This section of the trail follows a single road as it climbs over a mountain and down the other side. We leave behind a village, and enter cultivated plantations that transition to pastures and thick forests. Opportunities to acquire food or supplies are unreliable, but intermittent streams provide water. Aside from wildlife brave enough to approach the road, and the rare vehicle or villager, this is a section of solitude and serenity, with lush slopes where the only sounds are the streams and our footsteps.

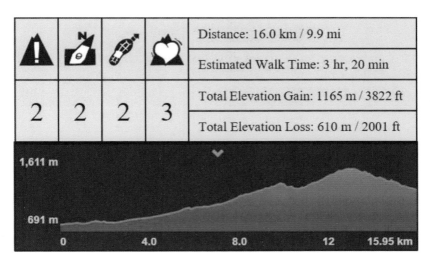

⚠	🧭	🥾	❤	Distance: 16.0 km / 9.9 mi
				Estimated Walk Time: 3 hr, 20 min
2	2	2	3	Total Elevation Gain: 1165 m / 3822 ft
				Total Elevation Loss: 610 m / 2001 ft

The white arrow points in the direction of El Camino de Costa Rica

Km 0: Humo de Pejibaye

The bridge into Humo de Pejibaye leads to a T-intersection where a sign points left to Refugio de Vida Silvestre El Copal. This protected land, and the adjacent greenhouse, are along our path. Smoother pavement proceeds up the hill to the right, but this leads through the town, and we avoid it. We approach the forest on Route 408, the conditions of which gradually diminish as we proceed left after the bridge.

First we cross another, smaller bridge that is simple concrete, with no pedestrian alternative. The rough pavement of Route 408 ascends almost immediately to the right. In 200 meters, we veer left onto a downhill slope through sugarcane fields. The terrain on our left drops steeply to Río Pejibaye. Earthen embankments line the right side of the road. Side paths and small trails lead into the fields, but we remain on the pavement. The homes and farm facilities here are part of the village of Taus. We continue for more than 2 kilometers through this community before passing Centro de Educación Ambiental Taus. A few hundred meters beyond this building, the pavement curves to the right. After another 400 meters, the road becomes gravel.

We begin an ascent: sometimes it is steep, sometimes gradual. In 1.6 kilometers, where purple flowers line the road, our altitude provides a wide view of the nearby valley. We encounter a brief descent one kilometer farther down the road, then climb to the entrance of El Copal. Only a sign on the left side of the road indicates when we reach this site, which is home to a wildlife refuge, and an option for lodging, but only if confirmed in advance. To enter, we pass through a gate of barbed wire and climb the hill on a gravel road to see the greenhouse on the far side. Beyond the greenhouse, the road continues to the lodging facility. However, El Camino de Costa Rica bypasses the refuge and remains on Route 408.

Km 6.2: Refugio de Vida Silvestre El Copal

After El Copal, the trail continues to ascend. Within a few kilometers, the conditions of the road diminish. To our right, a small shrine behind a barbed wire fence marks this transition from gravel to rough dirt. A long shed stands nearby, but otherwise, the view is consistent. Discernable landmarks are rare. We are surrounded by steep ridges, dense forests, and occasional pastures and farms. Only intermittent streams crossing our path distinguish one section of the trail from the next.

Tiny shrines sometimes stand beside the trail

The climb continues for 4.5 kilometers, interrupted by a brief descent that precedes the highest elevation in this section. We pass through the village of Tausito, dispersed so broadly and hidden so well among the slopes and woods that it would be difficult to notice if not for the streetlights. Beyond the summit of the road, we have glimpses of the wide valley carved by Río Orosi, which is home to Parque Nacional Tapantí. From here we follow switchbacks downhill for 3.4 kilometers.

Homes in the jungle are hidden among the trees, often perched on steep slopes

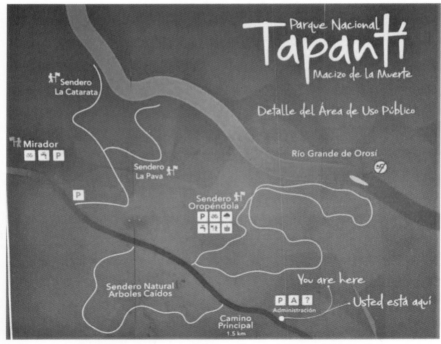

The hiking routes available at Parque Nacional Tapantí

As we approach the floor of the river valley, a wooden sign at an intersection to our left invites us to Parque Nacional Tapantí. The smiling tapir on the sign says, "Bienvenidos," although the park is known for Macizo de la Muerte: the Massif of Death. To reach the park itself, we take the left turn. El Camino de Costa Rica continues to the right, although this section ends here. The next market is in a village 3 kilometers farther along to the right, and more lodging options and resources are in the town 3 kilometers beyond that. The majority of this additional distance is paved.

Km 16.0: Parque Nacional Tapantí (Intersection)

If we turn left off Route 408, and divert from El Camino de Costa Rica, the Parque Nacional Tapantí entrance is 1.9 kilometers down a gravel road. After the first 800 meters we pass the entrance to Hacienda Ganadera on our right, which offers meals and lodging. Trees cover the majority of the road past this point.

Parque Nacional Tapantí features four main hiking trails, the longest and most difficult of which is 3 kilometers. Swimming along the river is prohibited, but there are spots for picnics. These offer a good chance of seeing animals that choose to avoid areas with more frequent vehicle traffic.

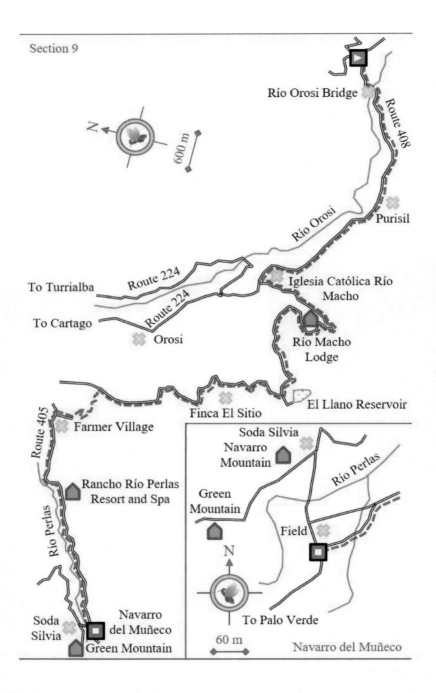

Section 9: Tapantí – Navarro del Muñeco

Río Orosi seen from the pedestrian bridge

This section passes closest to Cartago and San José, but begins near a national park, and ends at a tiny community tucked in a narrow valley. Beyond the city of Orosi and its surrounding towns, which stray a few kilometers from the trail, opportunities to purchase supplies and address other needs grow limited. There are also long stretches that follow major roads without substantial overhead protection. And with so much to see and do here, it is easy to justify lingering for an extra day.

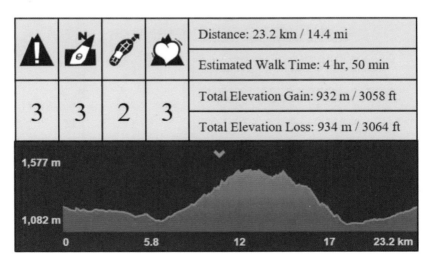

⚠ 3	🧭 3	👟 2	❤ 3	Distance: 23.2 km / 14.4 mi
				Estimated Walk Time: 4 hr, 50 min
				Total Elevation Gain: 932 m / 3058 ft
				Total Elevation Loss: 934 m / 3064 ft

Km 0: Parque Nacional Tapantí (Intersection)

On Route 408, at the intersection where a side road leads to Parque Nacional Tapantí, we veer right, away from the park. We soon cross a concrete slab bridge. After another 600 meters, we reach the large metal bridge over Río Orosi, and use the pedestrian passageway on the left to avoid vehicles. Once across, we meet pavement that continues in varying conditions, and several smaller bridges, on the way to the village of Purisil. The steep slope of a ridge lines the path on our left. Thick reeds and sugarcane grow in the river valley on our right. Where the ridge recedes from the road, we cross one more concrete bridge and see the Purisil sports field on the left.

Km 3.1: Purisil

The church and central field of Purisil

Tucked into a pocket among the ridges of the Talamanca Range, Purisil is almost small enough for us to see entirely across it. As we pass the central field, the church and school are visible if we look back to the left. The first building we encounter at the far end of the field is the bus stop, followed by Minisuper Purisil. This is the first place to purchase food since leaving Humo de Pejibaye, and their small selection is more than sufficient to provide an energy boost.

Continuing past Purisil, we remain on the pavement of Route 408 and cross more small bridges on the way to Río Macho. As the valley widens, industrial-scale farms fill the fields. After a kilometer, the ridge on our right diminishes, and Irazú Volcano appears in the distance. The city of Cartago crawls up the southern slopes of this active volcano, one of the highest in Costa Rica. This section of El Camino de Costa Rica brings us closest to Cartago: it is accessible by taxi or bus from Orosi. Cartago is also the most expedient city from which to access San José while on the trail, since the trip would not require navigating around high mountains or protected forests.

After we travel 2.3 kilometers beyond Purisil, our road curves to the right, but a gravel road continues into the fields to the left. The gravel road leads to Hacienda Orosi, a restaurant centered around natural hot springs for swimming, and Finca Queveri, a horse ranch with lodging and a restaurant at the top of a hill. The sign for Finca Queveri at this intersection is visible when approaching from Orosi on Route 408, but once on this side road, there are plenty of markers for additional guidance. The Hacienda is 300 meters from this curve, but reaching Finca Queveri requires following signs up a hill for 3.4 kilometers. However, with prior coordination, the lodging operators can arrange transportation to and from the trail by car, or on horseback.

The trail slopes downhill on Route 408, away from Hacienda Orosi

We continue along Route 408 for another 500 meters to a large concrete bridge, and follow a leftward curve in the road. Past this arc we arrive at a T-intersection, where Iglesia Católica de Río Macho stands on our left. However, the more obvious structure is the tremendous power station operated by the Instituto Costarricense de Electricidad (ICE). Standing at this intersection, we are on the outskirts of the city of Orosi, in the neighborhood of Río Macho. The trail turns left and climbs a slope into a colorful neighborhood, passing between the church and the power station. If we instead continue straight to Orosi, the center of the city is 3 kilometers farther along; first on Route 408, then on Route 224. A taxi or bus may come by to provide transportation into Orosi.

Orosi: The city of Orosi is not directly on El Camino de Costa Rica, but offers resources like a Banco Nacional with an ATM next to a supermarket, a Western Union, medical services, restaurants, and lodging. From the city plaza, most establishments for hikers are within 500 meters. To reach Orosi from Iglesia Católica de Río Macho, we divert from El Camino de Costa Rica and follow Route 408 for another kilometer, to where it connects with Route 224. At the intersection with a Mobil gas station on our right, we turn left, then right almost immediately. The yellow dividing line in the center of the road confirms we are on Route 224, and the increase in shops and homes indicates that we are approaching the city. Signs direct us to various places to eat and sleep, but some destinations are off the main road. Prior coordination with lodging providers is recommended for assistance with directions and transportation. Some hotels can also support day trips to Parque Nacional Tapantí, or to Cartago, home of the Basílica de Nuestra Señora de Los Ángeles. This sanctuary is dedicated to the patron saint of Costa Rica: La Negrita, the Virgin of Los Angeles. Other available activities include tours of local coffee farms, and samplings of rum manufactured locally from the sugarcane grown in the valley.

Km 6.4: Río Macho

To continue on El Camino de Costa Rica from Iglesia Católica de Río Macho, we ascend a paved road for 600 meters, passing between tidy, brightly painted homes. The fresh asphalt, sturdy fences, and sidewalk convey the quality of life enjoyed in this community. Leaving the houses behind, we reenter an area of dense foliage. A break in the greenery after 400 meters allows access to the river, and beyond this gap we veer left at a Y-intersection. The fork to the right leads up a steep hill to Río Macho Lodge, one of the few places we can sleep in this area within walking distance from the trail, and the last before we cross over the hills to Navarro del Muñeco.

As we climb the wide paved road, we remain on the sidewalk wherever possible. Fields and orchards fill every available section of the diminishing valley on our right. On our left, a few rows of trees separate us from the stream. Near the end of the remaining 1.4 kilometers of pavement, we find Iglesia Calle Sanchez on our left, and then step onto the gravel access road that leads up to El Llano Reservoir.

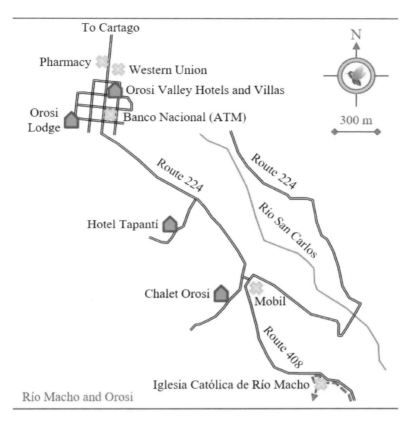

To Cartago

Pharmacy

Western Union

Orosi Valley Hotels and Villas

Banco Nacional (ATM)

Orosi Lodge

N

300 m

Route 224

Route 224

Río San Carlos

Hotel Tapantí

Chalet Orosi

Mobil

Route 408

Iglesia Católica de Río Macho

Río Macho and Orosi

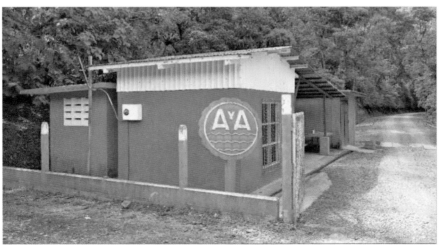

An AyA building marks the turn near El Llano Reservoir

Instituto Costarricense de Acueductos y Alcantarillados manages El Llano Reservoir, and may have the gate locked at the T-intersection 3 kilometers up the hill from Iglesia Calle Sanchez. This gate controls vehicle entry to additional resource management stations. If it is closed, we can step over the low concrete wall next to the barrier and continue. We take this right turn, and pass the blue AyA building marked with bold white letters. We are at the highest elevation along this trail section, which is why the aquafer is just a few hundred meters down the opposite road.

From the slopes we look down onto Río Perlas...

We remain on the access road past the AyA building for more than a kilometer, and pass another gate. A side road leads to Finca El Sitio, but we ignore the trails to the left that lead up to the farm. We also pass side trails that would take us back down the hill to the right. After crossing a concrete erosion barrier, the trail curves around to the left before making a sharp right turn 700 meters later. At the next swinging gate, we can use the pedestrian gap to continue straight up a small incline. This leads to a concrete waterway from which we can see the ridge across the valley. We can also see the paved road running along the valley floor.

... and Route 405

The trail follows the waterway down for 600 meters. We stop under a patch of trees where the waterway widens and grows steeper. Looking back to our left, we find a farm trail that takes us into the coffee fields that cover these rolling hills. We zigzag west among the crops for nearly a kilometer before two hairpin turns – first right, then left – help us face north. Looking straight down the trail, we cover the final 400 meters to Route 405 / Puente Negro. This stretch brings us past a row of rustic homes where farm workers live with their families. Beyond the last house on the left, we stand on pavement at a T-intersection, and turn left.

Approaching Route 405, the trail passes a row of small houses

Route 405 takes us the remaining 4.8 kilometers to Navarro del Muñeco, which members of the community often refer to simply as Muñeco. The road is paved and in good condition for much of the distance, and gently ascends the entire way. The valley narrows as the elevation increases, until farmers can no longer use the land. The last patch of crops is one kilometer from the farm village where we came down from the aquafer. Here a road turns right, crosses a stream, and steeply ascends the far ridge towards Cartago. We continue straight, and keep right after another 100 meters to stay near the water. A small gap in the reeds allows access to the river, and then we reach the gates of Rancho Río Perlas Resort and Spa. The road conditions for the 2.8 kilometers beyond Rancho Río Perlas are less consistent, but we still follow Route 405 to where it ends at the village of Muñeco.

At the entrance to Muñeco, a river flows directly across the road ahead of us, but this is not a problem. Passing vehicles drive through this waterway without hesitation, over a shifting layer of polished rocks. They emerge via the sloped embankment on the far side of the river. However, there is another way for pedestrians, visible to our left. Looking upstream along the riverbank, we notice a small dirt path that leads to a footbridge over the water. This is the way, and once across, we are in Muñeco.

The road crosses a waterway, but there is a narrow bridge nearby

Km 23.2 Navarro del Muñeco

At the T-intersection where a wooden fence wraps the terrain in front of us, we reach the end of this section. Across the field to our right sits the local church, near the main road into town. The field itself is lined with tires and trees colorfully painted in the blue, white, and red of the Costa Rican flag. It bears mentioning that due to the high slopes surrounding Muñeco, wireless internet connectivity is essentially unavailable here. One spot that may provide reception is the intersection by the school across from the village field, but even here the connection is unreliable.

When facing the wooden fence, the trail leading west from Muñeco continues up the hill to our left, but lodging is available to our right, past the school. To find a place to stay, and a small market, we head to the right, and soon reach another river. The bridge here consists of large concrete slabs meant to support vehicles, so we check for oncoming traffic before crossing. On the far side, we come to an intersection with a left turn, where a bus stop sits on the right. The house across from this bus stop includes Soda Silvia, which has limited hours but offers a small selection of snacks and beverages. At the turn up the road to the left here, painted wooden signs list options for lodging. The first, in 100 meters, is Navarro Mountain, up a steep hill through a gate to the right. The second, on the left after 300 meters, is Green Mountain.

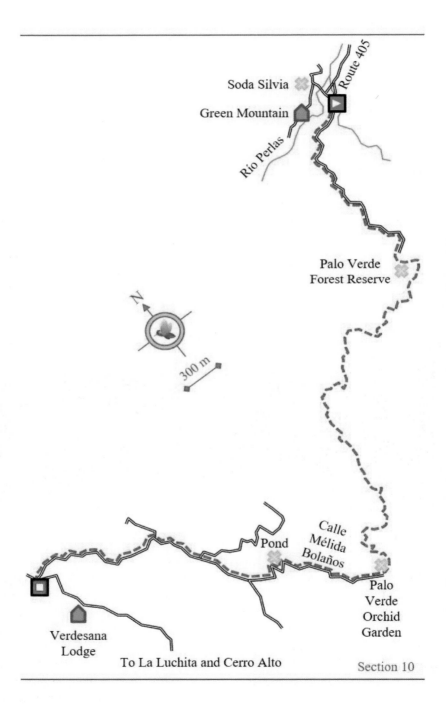

Soda Silvia

Green Mountain

Route 405

Río Perlas

Palo Verde
Forest Reserve

N

300 m

Calle
Mélida
Bolaños

Pond

Palo
Verde
Orchid
Garden

Verdesana
Lodge

To La Luchita and Cerro Alto

Section 10

106

Section 10: Navarro del Muñeco – Palo Verde

Welcome to the cloud forest at Palo Verde Forest Reserve

In this section, the trail leads up to a ridge, then follows it south until crossing to the far slope. The ridgeline passes through Palo Verde Forest Reserve, which is a protected, private cloud forest that stretches over the mountain slopes. The environment is similar to the dense forest found in the indigenous territory near Las Brisas. A guide is required through the Reserve, and can be requested from the owners in advance to meet hikers at the entrance.

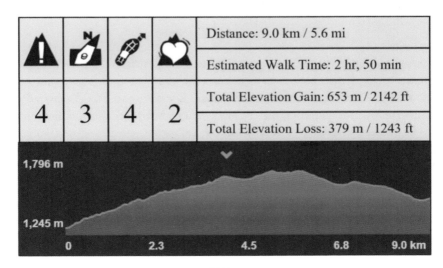

⚠	🧭	👟	❤	Distance: 9.0 km / 5.6 mi
				Estimated Walk Time: 2 hr, 50 min
4	3	4	2	Total Elevation Gain: 653 m / 2142 ft
				Total Elevation Loss: 379 m / 1243 ft

Although challenging, the relatively short distance of this section allows us to combine it with Section 11, if we start at a reasonable time and maintain a steady pace. If we stop at Verdesana Lodge in Palo Verde, there are comfortable cabins available on a manicured hillside with a view of forested slopes from the restaurant on site. Whether or not we stop there, the next market along the trail is approximately 20 kilometers away, in the village of La Luchita. Therefore, before departing Muñeco, we should have supplies and a plan for the next two sections.

A view of Navarro del Muñeco from the road leading to Palo Verde

Km 0: Navarro del Muñeco

From the path that led past the field on the way into Muñeco and ended at a T-intersection, we take the gravel road that leads uphill to the left. For the next hundred meters, the road follows an S-curve to the right and then the left, past a few houses and side trails. Then the trail becomes steeper and transitions to rough pavement. At 500 meters up the hill from the field, we leave the village behind us and can look to the right for a view of the valley. About one kilometer farther along, a few hundred meters past a devious false summit, the pavement transitions to a narrow dirt trail lined with thick foliage on both sides. The trail surface alternates between dirt and slick red mud, with occasional sections still paved to help vehicles on the steeper slopes. The sounds of birds and wildlife fill our ears as we approach the edge of the forest.

About 600 meters beyond the false summit, or 300 meters from the first breaks in the pavement, we arrive at a Y-intersection. Some online mapping tools identify this location as Sanctuary Farm Eco Community, but there are no signs. Overgrown vehicle tracks lead to the right, and a more visible red dirt road leads uphill to the left. We take the left road, into denser woods. In under 200 meters, the trail splits again, this time blocked in both directions by a barbed wire fence. Fortunately, there is a pedestrian gap in the fence to the right, so we can continue towards the sign that identifies the entrance to Palo Verde Reserva, a protected cloud forest. This is the recommended location to connect with a guide from the team that manages the land.

Km 1.9: Palo Verde del Guarco Forest Reserve

A colorful local resident of the cloud forest

In just over 100 meters past the cloud forest entrance, we find the first of several places where the trail is only a muddy canal with an eroded central gulley washed slick by runoff from rain. Careful observation often reveals drier footpaths that veer around the muddiest areas and reconnect to the main trail after a few meters. These are common in the forest, but we must remain vigilant if choosing these deviations, and not stray too far from the primary trail. There are few natural landmarks to aid in navigation here, and visibility is limited to one hundred meters at the most, due to the dense plant life. If ever unsure about the trail, it is best to turn around and return to an identifiable location to reset, rather than continue into the unknown.

Yellow arrows help identify the trail

Going forward, every incline up or down becomes slippery mud that requires careful footing. Nature quickly reclaims the trail: in places where fallen trees appear to block the way ahead, it is most likely a recent, natural occurrence. At these spots, we must peer through the barriers to see if the trail continues on the far side. In some places a small diversion will lead around the blockage. If not, we must climb, crawl, or push our way through the obstacles.

A rare view through the canopy reveals an adjacent slope

A sign is posted on a tree 400 meters past the barbed wire fence where we entered the cloud forest. It reads "Bosque Protegido," and beyond it we encounter a stretch of level, well-maintained trail. An audible river rumbles up from the valley on our right as we follow the side of a hill. After descending to a stream crossing, we see a yellow arrow across the water, pointing to the left. Following this arrow leads along the waterline. However, the trail appears to ascend the slope directly to our front. Both options are effective. The lower path requires pushing through brush before turning right and climbing the slope. The straight path ascends and then turns left, parallel to the stream at a higher elevation. From where these two variants reconnect, another yellow arrow appears in less than 100 meters, and points further uphill.

Fallen leaves and mud can create a slippery trail

We continue past a valley concealed by the trees on our right, and arrive at a pair of curves that both lead in the same direction. The closer curve to the right is more overgrown, and leads down to the valley. We choose the second, also to the right, which takes us over a break in the ridge. Now we have a valley to our left, and any gap in the trees allows us to see the opposing hills. Those slopes are also blanketed by protected natural forest, which illustrates how much of Costa Rica appeared before the clearing of terrain for farming and development.

Just over 100 meters from the transition across the ridge, a yellow arrow points up the hill to the right. After 300 more meters, another yellow arrow provides the same guidance. The trail narrows to the width of one person: on the left, a wall carved from the earth; on the right, a downhill slope. We continue for nearly a kilometer before another major mud ascent, but the terrain up this climb appears almost carved into steps. After ascending a few meters, we turn right at one yellow arrow, and then left at the next. This leads down a more defined trail to a small creek. On the far side, we take another left turn, guided by a yellow arrow up similar steps. After scrambling along through this stretch of red mud, a yellow arrow points to the right, and we follow it to level ground. The road widens, the trees separate, and we emerge onto a gravel road. The small cabin on our right confirms that we have exited the denser woods.

One of the colorful homes along Calle Mélida Bolaños

Leaving the cabin 100 meters behind us, we arrive at a T-intersection with a yellow arrow pointing downhill to the right. This path takes us across a small stream to another T-intersection and another right turn. Just beyond the gate ahead of us, we see a wide, sloping valley lined with farms and colorful ranch homes. A pedestrian passageway allows us to pass to the right of the gate, near a covered sign for Palo Verde Orchid Garden. But we are just entering the expansive region of Palo Verde. The slopes of the ridges around us are part of the community, but we have another three kilometers of road to cover before reaching the conclusion of this section. We begin on Calle Mélida Bolaños, which leads down from the forest.

Km 5.9: Calle Mélida Bolaños

The gravel road ahead of us slopes downhill for nearly a kilometer. Many homes here have descriptive names like Quintas Palo Verde and Quinta Linda Vista on their outer gates. Bright flowers and red-leafed plants line private roads leading into adjacent farms. Most of these properties have been family-owned for multiple generations, but environmental protection regulations now prohibit the clearing of original forests. With limited options for expansion, farm owners found other ways to develop their territories, including the aesthetic landscaping visible from the trail. One local landowner, José, is responsible for management of the entire 692 hectares of Palo Verde Forest Reserve. He can often be found surveying the area to ensure the natural forests maintain their protected status.

A shaded spot to stop and rest

Where the downhill slope concludes, a stream flows under the trail into a small pond on our right, which features enhancements similar to those emplaced elsewhere by the local residents. We see covered benches next to a fountain that circulates the water in this pond. The setting is dramatically different from the muddy tracks through the dense jungle behind us. This is a peaceful place to rest and resupply on water, but we must remain respectful, as it is private property.

From the pond, we ascend on the gravel road past more private homes for 300 meters, to another gate across the trail. Here also there is a pedestrian passageway to the right of the gate, but we must mind the barbed wire and protect our equipment and clothing. Beyond this gate, we turn right and approach a view down the long axis of a valley where the occasional home decorates pastures dotted with patches of trees. Rounding a curve, the city of Cartago is visible on a distant mountainside. If the clouds separate, we can also see the domed top of Irazú Volcano. Where the trail splits, we remain on the gravel road as it curves downhill to the left. As the trail becomes steeper, we step onto pavement that brings us down to a chasm widened over time by a river. Rising out of the gulley, we cover the final 300 meters of this section, first leaving the pavement and then arriving at a T-intersection. The trail continues uphill to the left, but this is the end of the section.

Km 9.0: Palo Verde del Guarco

Cattle graze in the fields that surround the protected forest

Although this section concludes at an intersection of no particular significance, and without any resources clearly visible, there is lodging 500 meters farther along the trail, at Verdesana Lodge. A sign for this ranch points to the left, in the direction of El Camino de Costa Rica. Turning right at this intersection leads to the center of Palo Verde del Guarco, which is 1.8 kilometers off of the trail, further down a slope. Supplies are available in the small shops of the town, but diverting to it incurs an uphill climb back to the trail.

Continuing up the hill to the left, following the sign and making progress on the trail, we find the Verdesana Lodge entrance on our right after 500 meters. A pedestrian entrance is behind the left side of the main gate. This property includes multiple cabins with reliable hot water, and a restaurant that offers set meals. Due to the distance from the local community, meals are only available if scheduled in advance, to allow the staff time to prepare. Camping on the property is offered without reservations. An alternative is to continue on El Camino de Costa Rica all the way to Cerro Alto. There will be a market along the way, but not for 8.5 more kilometers.

A golden silk orb-weaver, or banana spider, in its web

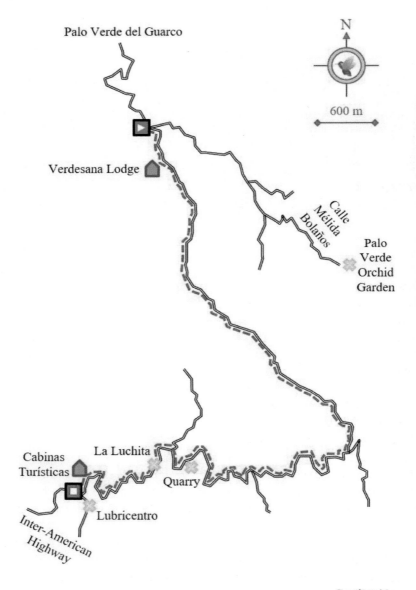

N

600 m

Palo Verde del Guarco

Verdesana Lodge

Calle
Mélida
Bolaños

Palo
Verde
Orchid
Garden

Cabinas
Turísticas

La Luchita

Quarry

Lubricentro

Inter-American
Highway

Section 11

116

Section 11: Palo Verde – Cerro Alto

The sunrise in Palo Verde illuminates distant volcanoes

Much of this section uses well-maintained roads, and offers views of distant peaks in all directions. The manageable elevation changes allow us to combine this section with Section 10, so long as we start at a reasonable time in the morning. This combination is advantageous since there are no shops along the trail from the Palo Verde Forest Reserve until the final approach to Cerro Alto. Just before this section ends, we can purchase food and beverages at a roadside store.

⚠️	🧭	👣	❤️	Distance: 10.0 km / 6.2 mi
				Estimated Walk Time: 3 hr, 10 min
2	2	2	3	Total Elevation Gain: 928 m / 3045 ft
				Total Elevation Loss: 324 m / 1063 ft

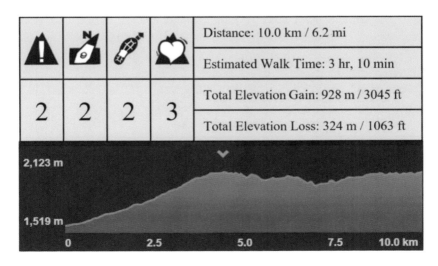

The view from inside a cabin at Verdesana Lodge

Km 0: Palo Verde del Guarco

This section begins at the T-intersection where the road from Palo Verde Forest Reserve ended. A sign here points left towards Verdesana. The Verdesana Lodge is on El Camino de Costa Rica, so we take this left turn and ascend on a wide dirt road. The gate for Verdesana is 500 meters up this hill, on our right. Lodging is available here, but meals at the restaurant require prior coordination to allow the staff time to procure fresh ingredients. Verdesana Lodge is one of many ranches in the area, although few provide lodging or amenities.

We gain elevation for another 3.5 kilometers without encountering a major turn or intersection. The side roads we pass lead either down the slope of a ridge, or into a private ranch, so we ignore them. As we climb, the shade of a particularly large tree on our left provides a comfortable spot to rest and view the fields and hills that fade into the horizon. At the top of this incline, the trail remains relatively level until the end of this section. Another 800 meters leads to a side road on our left, but we continue straight into a series of S-curves that descend across the next kilometer.

On the far side of a small community, we descend through trees again, this time to a concrete slab bridge tucked beneath the canopy. Rising out of this gully, we follow the terrain as it curves to the left. The gravel road leads 600 meters around a ridge, to a quarry. From here, we cover 400 meters to a wide T-intersection and veer left. In 200 meters, we step onto pavement and enter the village of La Luchita.

At the top of a small rise, we spot two notable buildings on the left side of the trail. The first is Pulperia La Luchita, our first opportunity to purchase food and drinks since this section began. The second is Liceo Rural La Luchita. Past the shop and school, we exit this small mountain village. The clearest indicator that the community is behind us comes 500 meters beyond the store, at the end of the pavement.

Km 10.0: Cerro Alto

Again on a gravel road, we cover 400 meters and cross a concrete slab bridge. Another 400 meters brings us to the Cabinas Turísticas entrance, on the right. Each cabin here has an equipped kitchen, and sleeps either two or four guests. The restaurant serves a set menu for breakfast and dinner, and the staff can deliver dinners to the cabins. The restaurant and office area also offers internet access. This lodging opportunity is 200 meters from National Primary Route 2, which is also the Inter-American Highway and the main conduit through Cerro Alto. This section ends where the trail turns left onto the highway.

Red and white trail blazes appear on rocks, trees, street signs, and posts

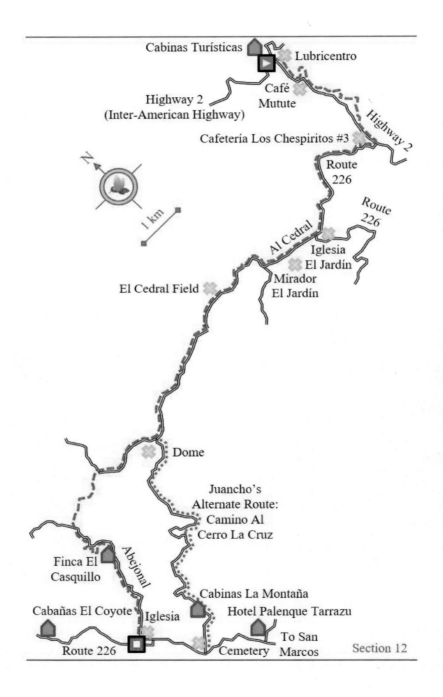

Cabinas Turísticas

Lubricentro

Highway 2
(Inter-American Highway)

Café
Mutute

Highway 2

Cafetería Los Chespiritos #3

Route
226

Route
226

N

1 km

Al Cedral

Iglesia
El Jardín

Mirador
El Jardín

El Cedral Field

Dome

Juancho's
Alternate Route:
Camino Al
Cerro La Cruz

Abejonal

Finca El
Casquillo

Cabinas La Montaña

Cabañas El Coyote

Iglesia

Hotel Palenque Tarrazu

To San
Marcos

Route 226

Cemetery

Section 12

120

Section 12: Cerro Alto – San Pablo de Leon Cortes

Sunrise at Cerro Alto

This section includes the highest elevation on the trail, followed by a long ridge through vast coffee plantations. From these heights we can see rows of mountains to the north and south when the cloud cover lifts. Closer to the city, we encounter several organic farms that promote sustainable agriculture. San Pablo de Leon Cortes is also the last urban area on the trail before we reach the Pacific, so whatever is required for the remaining sections should be gathered there in anticipation of the journey.

⚠	🧭	🧴	❤	Distance: 18.8 km / 11.7 mi
				Estimated Walk Time: 3 hr, 50 min
2	3	2	3	Total Elevation Gain: 406 m / 1332 ft
				Total Elevation Loss: 992 m / 3255 ft

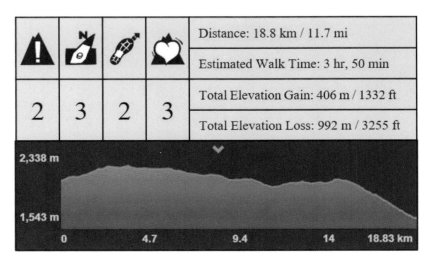

Km 0: Cerro Alto

Starting with a left turn onto the Inter-American Highway, we pass the Lubricentro car repair shop and follow the paved highway, using caution to avoid vehicles. Drivers are not looking for pedestrians here. After a kilometer, we complete a hairpin turn and spot Café Mutute on our right. The peak of Cerro Dragon comes into view, but we watch for a side road to the left. From Café Mutute, we travel 300 meters and find this gravel road, which takes us up a ridge adjacent to the highway. By passing through the neighborhood here, we skip a portion of the paved road. We avoid entrances to homes along this narrow sideroad, and reach its summit after 1.1 kilometers of gentle climbing. On the way down to where we reconnect with the pavement, we veer right at intersections and then turn left once again onto the Inter-American Highway. From this turn, we proceed 400 meters and arrive at Cafetería Los Chespiritos #3.

Km 3.7: Cafetería Los Chespiritos #3

The snack shop at Cafeteria Los Chespiritos #3 complements the buffet

This cafeteria sits just past a Mobil service station at the busy intersection of Highway 2 and Route 226. This intersection is noteworthy as the highest point along El Camino de Costa Rica, at 2347 meters, even though the view consists only of a grassy slope, stretches of pavement, and a rest stop parking lot.

The cafeteria itself is one of a chain in Costa Rica: Los Chespiritos #1 and #2 are farther south on Highway 2. The establishments are named for a Mexican sketch comedy show created by and starring Roberto Gomez Bolaños. His stage name was Chespirito – Little Shakespeare – and he was renowned throughout Latin America as a comedian, screenwriter, director, and producer. However, none of this history is indicated by the outward appearance or interior décor of this pay-by-item buffet and market. Inside, tables can accommodate 20 customers, and the service is quick. Meals are hot and satisfying, with fruit and other snacks available from the store.

Valley floors are dedicated to farming, and houses cover the slopes

Where Highway 2 and Route 226 meet, we turn right and follow the paved road as it twists into the town of Jardin de Dota. Local artisans here specialize in ceramics and woodcrafts, which can purchased if homes and shops are open. After 3.1 winding kilometers, we pass between bus stops on both sides of the street, and arrive at a Y-intersection. The building on our left is Iglesia El Jardín, but we veer onto the pavement to the right, away from Route 226. We are now on Al Cedral. Its paved segment ends after 400 meters, at a 4-way intersection dominated by a red and white radio tower on the left. Straight ahead, the road becomes dirt. We continue down this dirt trail, flanked by wild grapes. Soon we are among large ranches, one of which is Mirador El Jardín. Its gate appears 400 meters past the end of the pavement, on the left. Pulperia Alex is just past this gate, offering a limited selection of food and supplies.

Beyond Pulperia Alex, the dirt road splits at a wide T-intersection, and we turn right towards the town of El Cedral. The road becomes paved after 700 meters, which signifies the start of the town. We soon see Abastecedor Arroyo, a small snack shop designed to suggest a log cabin, and then pass between the village church to our left and the Escuela el Cedral to our right. The sports field is just beyond the school, lined with a stone wall. Across the street sits the largest market in the village, to capitalize on the audience for sports, festivals, and other events. After nearly a kilometer, the pavement transitions to broken asphalt and then dirt as we leave the town.

Mountain ranges fade into the horizon

A couple hundred meters after the start of this dirt road, we take the path at a Y-intersection that remains high on a ridge. From this elevation, we can see details of life on the adjacent slopes, whose ridges parallel our own. The curling mountain ranges are home to energy-generating windmills that rise above the neatly planted but undulating fields. When a paved side road intersects our dirt trail from the right, we skip it and continue straight. Another 1.5 kilometers beyond the paved side street, we ignore a trail leading downhill, and continue our ascent. Up ahead, a tree-covered dome fills our view. The canopy closes above us, and we take the path that circles the terrain to the right when the road splits at the base of the dome.

The trail here consists of the same red earth that creates a natural wall to our left. It becomes slick when traveled on frequently. After 700 meters, we round the dome, and veer left for the next 2 kilometers. Across fields on our right we have a different view of the same ridges seen previously. The arc of our trail continues to trace around the ridge, then descends into San Pablo de Leon Cortes.

When this descent begins, we ignore the trail leading back and down to our right, and after 600 meters are rewarded with a view of the city in the valley below us. The rocky trail here is Abejonal Road, which grows steep as we approach the city. On the way, we avoid side trails that lead into plantations and private homes.

The owners of farms here incorporate sustainable agricultural practices into their operations. Many offer tours for those interested in learning more. One such farm is Finca El Casquillo, with its gate just around a right turn 1.3 kilometers from the last side trail. The owners let guests camp overnight. They provide several levels of accommodation, and offer a tour of the grounds. Finca El Casquillo is also part of a cooperative enterprise with other farms in the area, and can arrange tastings of honey, coffee, salad dressing, and other locally-produced goods.

Km 16.8: Finca El Casquillo

Outside the gate at Finca El Casquillo, a sign mounted to a tree informs us that the city is 2 kilometers down the hill. As we stroll down the rocky dirt road, homes and farms appear more frequently. After 1.2 kilometers, we see the black gate for the Café Los Cuarteles coffee processing facility on our right. A small wooden sign behind their entrance to the left welcomes guests and advertises honey-processed coffee, harvested from the surrounding hills and processed locally.

Camp surrounded by the forest at Finca El Casquillo

Around another turn, the road becomes paved, and the town appears in the valley. The street we are on is now Avenida 1. We follow it to its opposite end, at a T-intersection by Parque Central in the city. On the left corner of this intersection stands Iglesia San Pablo Apóstol. Ahead of us, a path leads 100 meters along the edge of the park to a taxi stand on the road through the center of town. This is Calle 2, along which we can find several shops, markets, a post office, and a bank with an ATM. In rural areas, most businesses only take cash, so this is the time to plan ahead for the next several days. That could mean purchasing supplies, or acquiring more of the local currency. The taxis can take us to lodging options within a few kilometers, but the end of Avenida 1 at the park and church is where this section concludes.

Km 19.1: San Pablo de Leon Cortes

The rooftops of San Pablo de Leon Cortes appear through the trees

San Pablo de Leon Cortes is one of the larger communities on the trail. Most of its resources for hikers can be found along Calle 2, which is a bypass for Route 226. From the taxi stand by the park, we see a Musmanni bakery across the street and Supermercado Liang to the right. Continuing past Supermercado Liang, we pass a variety of cafés, including one that offers Chinese-themed dishes. At the end of the Colegio Técnico Profesional, we can turn left and walk down Avenida 3 to the internet café, or continue one more block and turn down the street toward Con Gelados, the local ice cream shop. Farther along Calle 2, the Coope Supermercados, the farmacia, and a branch of Banco Nacional are all visible. Beyond the bank, private residences line Route 226 on the way to San Antonio. Cabañas Bongos and Cabañas El Coyote are 2 kilometers outside of San Pablo de Leon Cortes in this direction, but taxis can help cover that distance.

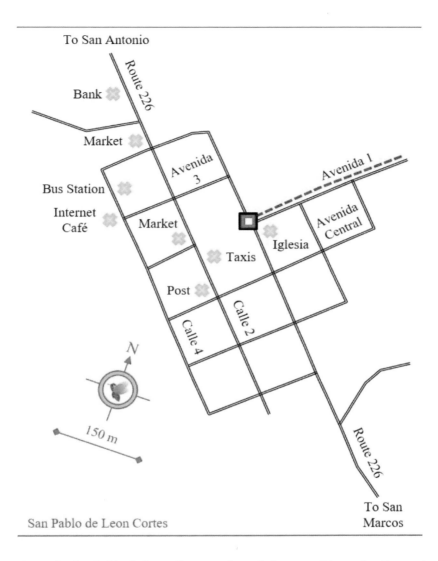

To San Antonio

Bank

Route 226

Market

Avenida 3

Bus Station

Internet Café

Market

Avenida 1

Avenida Central

Iglesia

Taxis

Post

Calle 4

Calle 2

N

150 m

Route 226

To San Marcos

San Pablo de Leon Cortes

From the San Pablo de Leon Cortes taxi stand, the post office and police station are within 100 meters to the left. This is the direction taxis will take if headed to hotels that are closer to San Marcos. It is also a convenient place for taxis to return to in the morning, if we decide to stay overnight somewhere outside of walking distance. Both Cabinas La Montaña and Hotel Palenque Tarrazu are within 3 kilometers of the park where the taxis stop, on the way to San Marcos. On the road out of town, there is a cemetery on the left and a service station on the right, just before a large intersection.

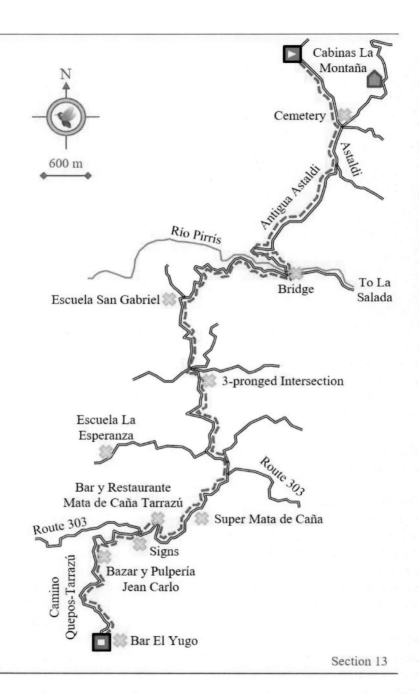

N

600 m

Cabinas La Montaña

Cemetery

Antigua Astaldi

Astaldi

Río Pirrís

Bridge

To La Salada

Escuela San Gabriel

3-pronged Intersection

Escuela La Esperanza

Route 303

Bar y Restaurante Mata de Caña Tarrazú

Super Mata de Caña

Route 303

Signs

Camino Quepos-Tarrazú

Bazar y Pulpería Jean Carlo

Bar El Yugo

Section 13

128

Section 13: San Pablo de Leon Cortes – Napoles

The cemetery on the edge of San Pablo de Leon Cortes

This portion of the trail requires frequent navigational decisions. The route proceeds across intersecting ridgeline roads, all leading through rows of crops. There are few places to acquire food or water, and almost no natural shade sources. Given the small size of the villages along the road, it is possible that the few shops encountered will be closed upon arrival. There are also significant elevation changes that add to the difficulty of this section. However, the ridges offer spectacular views down lush valleys where the tops of buildings rise just above the trees.

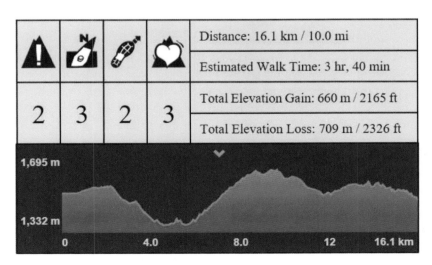

⚠ 2	🧭 3	🧭 2	❤ 3	Distance: 16.1 km / 10.0 mi
				Estimated Walk Time: 3 hr, 40 min
				Total Elevation Gain: 660 m / 2165 ft
				Total Elevation Loss: 709 m / 2326 ft

Km 0: San Pablo de Leon Cortes

San Pablo guards the church

Standing outside Iglesia San Pablo Apóstol, where Avenida 1 ends at Parque Central in the middle of San Pablo de Leon Cortes, we turn left and take the sidewalk to the southeast along Route 226. We leave the park behind on our right, and follow the paved road for 1.3 kilometers. As we exit the city, the sidewalk becomes crowded with pedestrians and cars entering and exiting the driveways along the road. Cementerio de San Pablo Leon Cortes appears on our left, its tiled tombs and shrines causing the hill to shimmer. Beyond the cemetery to the right, we see Estación de Servicio El Cruce, a gas station on the far side of a four-way intersection. To the left at this junction, a paved road leads 1 kilometer uphill to Cabinas La Montaña. Hotel Palenque Tarrazu is 1.4 kilometers ahead of us, in the town of San Marcos. El Camino de Costa Rica continues to the right on Astaldi, a wide and well-maintained dirt road. This is the path we take, keeping the gas station on our left as we proceed.

Markings appear along the trail here, in various shapes and colors that provide conflicting, contradictory guidance. These symbols apply to the numerous running, motorbike, and other races that occur in these hills. We follow only the red and white blazes, and the hummingbird symbols, for guidance. After 600 meters, we keep right at a Y-intersection that leads slightly uphill, and proceed on Antigua Astaldi. In another 100 meters, our road turns sharply to the right before curving around and descending on a ridge lined with side trails. We ignore these for the next kilometer, and are rewarded with an opening in the trees that provides views on both sides of the trail. Plantations and an assortment of orchards cover the hills to the north and west in shades of green. The city of San Marcos fills the eastern valley.

We maintain our current elevation for a few hundred meters before starting the descent to Río Pirrís. At a tight S-turn, we arc left and then around to the right, avoiding the road that leads back in the direction of San Marcos. From here, we reach the bottom of the descent. Grass grows thick due to the presence of the river.

Rustic farmhouses and small homes line the road on both sides. Creeks trickle across our path, flowing down from the hills and watering the crops. Around a corner, we arrive at a metal and concrete bridge just wide enough for a vehicle. This bridge takes us across Río Pirrís.

A pastoral vista seen from the bridge over Río Pirrís

Km 4.7: Río Pirrís

On the far side of the bridge over Río Pirrís, we step onto a dirt road at a T-intersection. The building on the left is Escuela Victor Campos Valverde. Beyond the school's field, the road becomes Calle El Salado, which leads 1.8 kilometers into the town of La Salada. We turn right, away from the school, and stay on the dirt road that follows the river. After 300 meters, a side trail cuts back uphill to the left, but we continue straight. We trace the curve of the river for another 700 meters before weaving up into the hills. The trail climbs for a kilometer to a multi-pronged intersection, but we ignore side trails and continue straight. In 400 meters, the trail curves gently to the right, and we spot the first few homes of San Gabriel. However, our road immediately veers left and uphill to a wide dirt T-intersection.

Km 7.5: San Gabriel

As we enter this village, we find Escuela San Gabriel next to a church on our right. Looking to our left, we see warehouses, a small shop, and a collection of rustic wooden homes along the edge of the road before a section of pavement. We turn left toward the pavement, and start to ascend. A sign for La Cumbre, a producer of specialty coffee, greets us on a gate after 500 meters, but this is not a café. We are in the hills of Tarrazú, at the elevation where this coffee is grown. Many residents of San Gabriel work in these hills, harvesting coffee beans. The refinement process continues in San Marcos, and the packaged product is shipped internationally.

Trails snake through the coffee fields so that farmers can access the crops

The pavement leads around tight turns and transitions to dirt across the next 700 meters before ending at a T-intersection, where we turn left. Directly in front of us sits a 3-pronged intersection. We take the gravel road leading to the right, and ignore narrow side trails that enter the fields. Our route widens on a ridge for 800 meters, then snaps around a hairpin turn to the left. Pausing to observe the ridges covered with coffee trees facilitates an understanding of the immense dedication to coffee production in the region, and the challenges of harvesting the beans. Steep dirt roads twist across the terrain to provide access to the fields, but our trail follows the ridge that curves to the right up ahead. From the hairpin left turn, we proceed in this direction another kilometer, to an intersection where a sharp left turn begins the descent to Mata de Caña. A gravel road crosses perpendicular to our direction of travel, and by turning right onto it we can just see Route 303 at the bottom of a slope. We continue and turn right on this paved road, which will lead us through the village.

Km 11.1: Mata de Caña

Storms occur regularly during the rainy season, along with rainbows

Route 303 is a main road through this area, but a sidewalk on the right side lets us avoid walking in the street. The village of Mata de Caña stretches along the road, with houses tucked among the trees on both sides of the ridge. Our first opportunity to purchase supplies is in 800 meters, just past a church, at the Super Mata de Caña. The church is on the right, and this supermercado is on the left as we transition to an ascent. Super Mata de Caña has groceries, hygiene items, and other supplies that are not available in Napoles. A smaller shop, Pulpería La Flor, sits on the right side of the road 400 meters farther along, with a pastoral image painted on the exterior but a limited selection inside. The sign for this shop is difficult to find, but the colorful murals, which reflect the lifestyle of the local people, are easy to identify.

Caught in the rain in Napoles.

Our ascent continues another 800 meters to a tight left turn around Bar y Restaurante Mata de Caña Tarrazú, with a wide view of the ridges we just traversed available from the parking lot. Inside its picket fence, the round restaurant also functions as a dance club, a place to watch sports on television, and a location for special events. Depending on lodging arrangements in Napoles, this restaurant may be the last opportunity to have a cooked meal along this section.

Signs begin to point to Quepos

There are multiple signs 300 meters beyond Bar y Restaurante Mata de Caña Tarrazú to ensure we veer left, off of Route 303, and onto a paved side road that twists along the left slope of a ridge. One points to Napoles: 3 km. The sign by the bus stop points to Napoles and Quepos. A large wooden sign advertises Rancho Turistico Mirador Buena Vista Tarrazú as 15 km down the road, almost as far as Naranjitto. The road itself is Camino Quepos-Tarrazú, but the views of San

Lorenzo and the surrounding mountains to the east are the attraction. From this altitude we can see lush slopes wrapped in clouds, fading into the horizon as we proceed.

After a kilometer of level terrain, we pass Bazar e Pulpería Jean Carlo to our left, with a colorful exterior but a limited supply of goods. The pavement then begins to break apart, until only asphalt and gravel remain. During our descent, buildings sporadically appear on the side of the road, but none of significance until we arrive in the center of Napoles. Most homes hide on the slopes. The primary intersection in this mountain village marks the end of this section.

Km 16.1: Napoles

In the center of this community, the road flares and splits into a Y-intersection. On our left, a set of playground equipment stands next to a building labeled as an Abastecedor and Bar El Yugo. The abastecedor offers snacks and some hygiene products, and the bar has limited hours. Even the employees at the shop acknowledge that more options and resources are available in Mata de Caña.

The right side of the Y-intersection in the town center leads uphill to a church, field, and school. Cabaña La Flor provides lodging near the school, but contact information for the establishment is not currently available. To continue on El Camino de Costa Rica we take the road that slopes downhill to the left, past the bar.

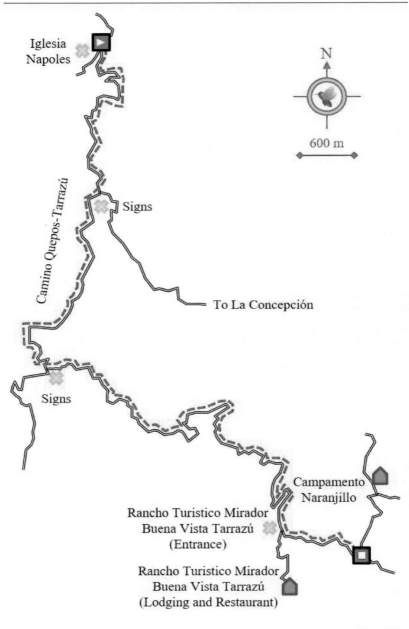

Iglesia
Napoles

Camino Quepos-Tarrazú

N

600 m

Signs

To La Concepción

Signs

Campamento
Naranjillo

Rancho Turistico Mirador
Buena Vista Tarrazú
(Entrance)

Rancho Turistico Mirador
Buena Vista Tarrazú
(Lodging and Restaurant)

Section 14

Section 14: Napoles – Naranjillo

The coastline is visible even on a hazy morning

With few intersections and a gentle descent, this section facilitates speed, but tempts hikers to stop often and appreciate the view. The Pacific Coast finally appears, while green mountain ridges flank the trail to the east.

⚠ 2	🧭 2	🍾 2	❤ 3	Distance: 13.0 km / 8.1 mi
				Estimated Walk Time: 2 hr, 50 min
				Total Elevation Gain: 444 m / 1457 ft
				Total Elevation Loss: 1148 m / 3766 ft

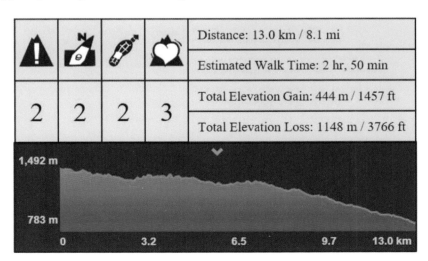

Km 0: Napoles

From the center of the small community of Napoles, we proceed to the left at a Y-intersection. The path to the right leads up to a school and a church before coming to an end. Our road is Camino Quepos-Tarrazú, which leads downhill on a gravel road with intermittent pavement. We avoid the side trails that lead into homes, farms, and fields, and remain on the wider road. After 500 meters we encounter a set of tight turns that weave back and forth across almost a kilometer before the trail continues to the south. We cross a canal and proceed along a smooth dirt road, with trees on the slope to our right.

Once the trail turns south, we cover another kilometer and emerge from the trees to find a wide view of the Pacific Ocean. The hills to our right slope down to a wide coastal plain blanketed with palm plantations and farmland. On clear days it is possible to spot thin stretches of the beach. To the left, a small farm at the edge of the road displays the only patch of exposed land on ridges otherwise covered in dense jungles that extend to the horizon.

Trees cover all the slopes but those closest to the road

A few hundred meters beyond this viewpoint, we see signs for Quepos and La Concepción at a Y-intersection that splits around a ridge. The arrow towards Quepos points to the right. We follow it, remaining on Camino Quepos-Tarrazú. This keeps the high side of the ridge on our left as we continue, which provides shade until the sun crests the terrain. Another 400 meters past this intersection, a boulder on the side of the road is marked with information about Rancho Turistico

Mirador Buena Vista Tarrazú. We note the distance to this restaurant and continue, mindful to step aside for vehicles and yield to mountain bikers.

The road maintains its elevation for 2.2 kilometers, and brings us to a hairpin turn with a particularly grand perspective on the coast. Over the course of another 600 meters, we finish a minor descent and face a collection of signs at an intersection where both options curve left. We choose the sharper, inside left turn, which diverts us from Camino Quepos-Tarrazú. This road will guide us to Rancho Turistico Mirador Buena Vista Tarrazú, where meals are available, and then to the town of Naranjillo, where we can find lodging for the night.

After we turn left at these signs, the trail gently ascends for a kilometer. We then begin a long, steady descent that will ultimately conclude at the base of the surrounding mountains, in the farmland on the coastal plains. As we continue, seasonal streams trickle across the trail from the adjacent slopes. Trees throw shade on the gravel and dirt road we use, as the trail traces the outline of the ridge. Each little curve with a stream enables us to pause and replenish our water, but the trees reduce visibility for drivers as they navigate the turns of the road. When resting in these spots, we remain careful to stay clear of traffic. We proceed in this fashion for 5 kilometers before arriving at the entrance to Rancho Turistico Mirador Buena Vista Tarrazú.

Km 12.0: Rancho Turistico Mirador Buena Vista Tarrazú

Secret streams are accessible via guided tours through the jungle

Clouds roll into the valleys that are visible through gaps in the trees

The side trail to this bar and restaurant requires a deviation of 900 meters from El Camino de Costa Rica, and most of that distance is uphill. At the top, the dining area overlooks all of the terrain leading into Quepos, and the Pacific Ocean beyond it. A member of the staff may not be present unless notified in advance of our arrival, but with coordination someone can meet us at the entrance or the dining area. Hosts can facilitate guided tours to waterfalls, or give educational presentations about how the farm operates.

Past the sign at the entrance to Rancho Turistico Mirador Buena Vista Tarrazú, we descend another kilometer to a set of hairpin turns. Just beyond them, a sign at an intersection points to Naranjillo on the left, and Esquipulas on the right. This section of the trail ends here, but we can find lodging in Naranjillo, in the valley to our left.

Water is often available adjacent to the trail

Km 13.0: Naranjillo

To reach the village of Naranjillo, we turn left and follow a steep descent for a kilometer. At the base of the hill, we turn left at a T-intersection and continue for 300 meters to Campamento Naranjillo. Prior arrangements are necessary for access to the camping area.

Some secrets of the forest are small

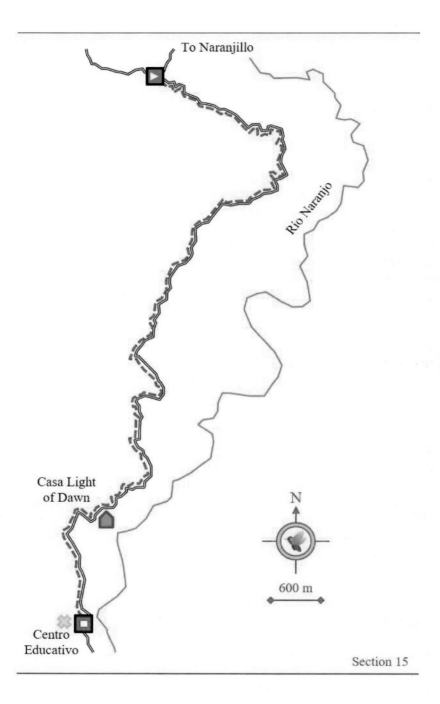

To Naranjillo

Río Naranjo

Casa Light
of Dawn

N

600 m

Centro
Educativo

Section 15

Section 15: Naranjillo – Esquipulas

A distant view of Parque Nacional Manuel Antonio

For the entire duration of this section, the trail follows one road that predominantly descends towards the Pacific. Streams flow down from higher elevations and cross the road on their way to the nearby river. Trees tower above the valley floors, and cast welcome shadows on our path.

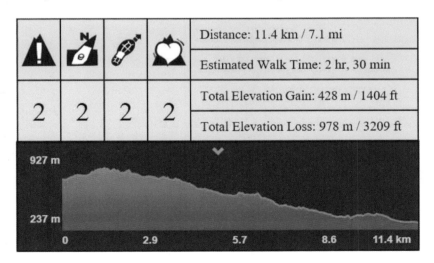

				Distance: 11.4 km / 7.1 mi
⚠	🧭	🥾	❤	Estimated Walk Time: 2 hr, 30 min
2	2	2	2	Total Elevation Gain: 428 m / 1404 ft
				Total Elevation Loss: 978 m / 3209 ft

Km 0: Naranjillo

At the intersection where a sign points left to Naranjillo and right to Esquipulas, we take the uphill road to the right. We gain elevation for the first 1.3 kilometers, then resume the long descent to the coastal plains that surround Quepos. When we first crest the highest stretch of this trail section, the slope to our left rolls into a broad, forested valley shaped by Río Naranjo. Across the river, the mountains are hidden under a thick canopy of treetops. Some of this territory can be farmed, but much of it is privately-owned natural forest that cannot be harvested due to government policies that protect the natural landscape. With the high slope on our right side, we do not have many views of the ocean as we descend, but sounds of the running river occasionally emerge from the trees.

Clouds embrace the hills when the temperature falls in the evening

For 6.4 kilometers, the scenery and the slope remain consistent. Then, for a moment, the water comes closer to the trail from our left. We cross a stream after another 700 meters, and will encounter many more trickles of water as we lose altitude. The trees encroach on both sides and provide us with shade in one of the last parts of El Camino de Costa Rica where unrestrained nature surrounds us.

The first structure we encounter is at a curve where a large gate blocks the entrance to a private home on our left. Many homes and farms are tucked under the trees along this road, to capitalize on the shade and the proximity to water. We follow the road to the right, and notice additional sporadic indicators of the upcoming village.

After 1.8 kilometers, we enter Esquipulas, a small community tucked under the trees around the road and river. On our left, the water purification facility for Naranjito, Villa Nueva, and Esquipulas reminds us that *El agua es vida.* "Water is Life." An excited, anthropomorphic drop of water opens its arms for us against the blue painted walls. We continue for 300 meters, across a concrete slab bridge, and end the section with the community sports field on our left and the local Centro Educativo on our right.

A homemade sign for a farm along the road

Km 11.4: Esquipulas

The Centro Educativo at Esquipulas

The local Centro Educativo is on the far side of a rustic barn, and hidden from view until we reach the southern end of the adjacent sports field. Two payphones with unreliable connectivity are on the left side of the road, across from the entrance to the center. Resources and lodging options are not consolidated locally here, due to the terrain, but can be found within 1.2 kilometers if we continue down the road to Esquipulas Rainforest Lodge.

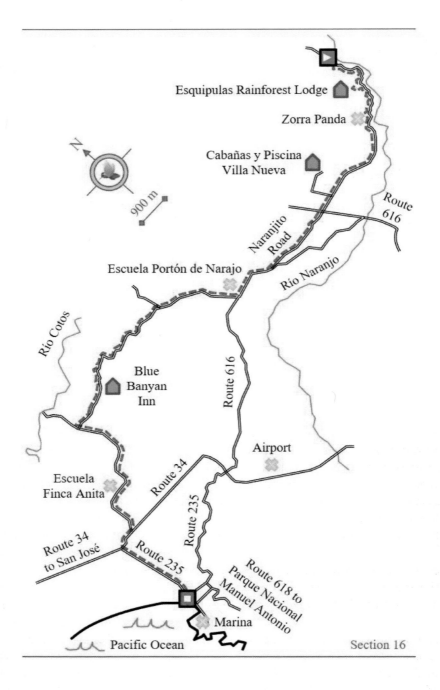

Esquipulas Rainforest Lodge

Zorra Panda

Cabañas y Piscina
Villa Nueva

Route
616

Naranjito Road

Escuela Portón de Narajo

Río Naranjo

Río Cotos

Blue
Banyan
Inn

Route 616

Airport

Escuela
Finca Anita

Route 34

Route 235

Route 34
to San José

Route 235

Route 618 to
Parque Nacional
Manuel Antonio

Marina

Pacific Ocean

Section 16

Section 16: Esquipulas – Quepos

The Pacific end of the trail is brightly identified

This stretch of the trail contains diversity that reflects much of what hikers encounter all along El Camino de Costa Rica, neatly compressed into a single section. After passing through farm villages, the trail enters a sprawling palm plantation where workers live in communities on the property. The palm trees end at a paved highway that leads directly into Quepos, taking us to the harbor and the end of the trail.

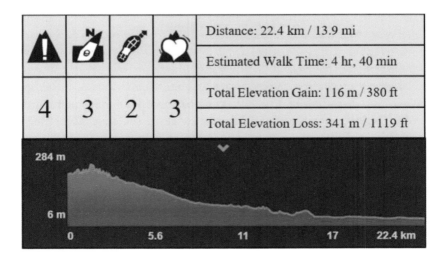

⚠	🧭	🪢	💚	Distance: 22.4 km / 13.9 mi
				Estimated Walk Time: 4 hr, 40 min
4	3	2	3	Total Elevation Gain: 116 m / 380 ft
				Total Elevation Loss: 341 m / 1119 ft

Km 0: Esquipulas

We begin on the gravel road that descends between the sports field and the Centro Educativo in Esquipulas. After 200 meters, we are across a concrete slab bridge and approaching the gate for Aguas De Tarrazú. The entrance to this scenic destination is on the left, but its sign is only visible after we pass the gate and look behind us. Inside, we can camp and explore the river and waterfalls.

In 500 meters, we leave behind the community of Esquipulas. An embankment presses against the road to our right, and the terrain drops off sharply to our left. For the next 2 kilometers, we wind along the side of this slope. Every curve to the left takes us past a view through the trees that shows the steepness of the descent to the river. Seasonal streams trickle across the road at these curves, and enable us to replenish our water in anticipation of higher temperatures on the coastal plain. Across the valley, the far ridges are hidden under an unbroken green canopy. These are the last glimpses of untouched wilderness we will see along El Camino de Costa Rica.

The gravel road we have followed ends at the Zorra Panda bar, on our right. The sign for this establishment features a smirking fox, or a *zorra*. From here, we step onto the smooth pavement of Naranjito Road. Gravel side roads lead off into the neighborhoods that line this street, but we ignore them and continue straight. Along the way, we see the sign for Villa Vanilla, a sustainable farm that offers tours and tastings of vanilla, cinnamon, and other spices grown on-site. Then, on our left, we spot the Super Villa Nueva market, followed by wide, level pastures. Opposite these fields we pass a row of colorful homes, many with decorative gates and brightly painted fences.

Km 5.1: Villa Nueva

Moving through the center of Villa Nueva, we pass Abastecedor La Amistad, the Plaza de Deportes de Villa Nueva, and the Centro Educativo in quick succession. At an intersection 100 meters beyond the plaza, we continue straight between the Iglesia Católica and a bus stop. Another 100 meters brings us to Minisuper Johancy #3, a large market where we can purchase supplies for the remainder of the trail.

When we are 700 meters beyond the supermarket, we reach a 4-way intersection but continue straight along the pavement. Here we use caution to avoid traffic, since there is no sidewalk and vehicles travel quickly to and from Naranjito. At a Y-intersection where a gravel road coming from the left intersects our route, we watch for merging and turning vehicles, and veer right onto Route 616. A sidewalk is available for much of the final 700 meters to the city.

Km 9.1: Naranjito

As we approach the main intersection in Naranjito, we pass markets, Bar La Deportiva, and a Panaderia y Reposteria. On our right, Escuela Portón de Naranjo and the sports field mark where we will turn. Past the school, across from Soda El Rinconcito, we turn right onto a road that transitions to packed dirt as it leads us north.

Pastures line the trail beyond Naranjito

Exiting Naranjito, we enter a neighborhood of ranch homes and farms, with names that evoke the nearby ocean, like Rancho Los Delfines and Rancho Pacifica, both of which we see on the right. Following along a fence with stone pillars, we arrive at a Y-intersection and take the left path toward Las Piscinas de Gabriel. For the next kilometer, we continue to veer left at Y-intersections on the descent to a valley floor. A concrete platform crosses a canal here, and then we pass a large warehouse on our right. Along this river valley are many private homes and farms that take advantage of the ample water supply. Industrial farm vehicles and cargo trucks also transit this road. It is best to step aside and provide them with space to maneuver.

Almost a kilometer beyond the bridge and the warehouse, a side road to the left leads to the Blue Banyon Inn and Kids Saving the Rainforest. These are sometimes abbreviated as BBI and KSTR on later signs, which will point back to this location. Down this side road we can find the reforestation and wildlife conservation area managed by the KSTR nonprofit organization, but instead we go straight, into a palm grove.

Km 14.8: Oil Palm Plantation

Colorful homes surround the central field in the plantation village

After 500 meters, we cross a canal into a large plantation of oil palms, following a wide gravel road. Deeper into the plantation, where a large painted rock advertises the Blue Banyon Inn, using letters painted in the appropriate color, we turn left. The road crosses a small concrete bridge in 600 meters, and along the way we may see harvesters at work. There are also access roads that lead between rows of trees: we avoid these distractions. We continue for another kilometer, to a village where the farmers live in wooden homes. Escuela Finca Anita is past this village, on the right, and the exit from the plantation is 600 meters beyond the school.

As we leave the plantation, the main dirt road narrows to a small concrete bridge that veers to the right, over a canal. We cross, and emerge onto National Primary Route 34. Cars move swiftly down this major street, so we turn right and remain on the sidewalk. Past a bus stop near Cementerio De Quepos, we approach a traffic circle. Aside from the road we followed to this point, there are two other roads that feed into the circle. Our path is the one to the left, headed south on Route 235, to Quepos. Once we find a safe place to cross the street, we know we are on the correct route when Supermercados BM is on our right.

We follow the road south from the traffic circle, using the intermittent sidewalk where available. Businesses line this road on both sides, so we must be alert for vehicles from every direction. There are no more turns on the trail, just a direct path to the finish. The final 500 meters of our hike lead across a bridge to a vibrant mosaiced sign that spells Quepos in large letters. It is here, on the boardwalk by a bay that opens to the Pacific Ocean, that El Camino de Costa Rica ends. It is possible to climb down the retaining wall along the waterfront and touch the water, concluding a walk across Costa Rica from sea to sea.

Km 22.4: Quepos

Locals and tourists stroll down the Quepos boardwalk, and lounge on the benches to watch the sunset. Small boats cruise in the bay, while jet skis bounce along the calm water. A forested slope descends to the water in the distance to the north. At the southern end of the bay, just beyond a small playground, sailboats sit in a harbor near Marina Pez Vela. This resort hotel is the most expensive, but most luxurious lodging conveniently available along the entire trail. Other accommodations and resources can be found on the streets of Quepos.

The first street we pass is Avenida 3, which takes us past a local tourism agency and a realty office on the way to the Serenity Boutique Hotel. Pizza Gabriela is also down this road, one of many places in town to regain some energy. The next street off Route 235 is Avenida 1, where we turn past China Quepos and El Gran Escape Restaurant towards the Hotel Malinche. At the far end of Avenida 1 we find a Banco Nacional with an ATM. If we instead remain on Route 235, there is a Best Western followed by Pops ice cream shop before the next street. The corner here is dominated by Supermarket Pura Vida, next to Farmacia Don Gerardo. If we turn at the supermarket onto Avenida Central, we come to the bus station, which is across from the taxi stand and a Banc Credomatic, which has an ATM. Further down Avenida Central is a Musmanni bakery and the Wide Mouth Frog hostel.

Parque Nacional Manuel Antonio is only a few kilometers south of Quepos. More lodging is available along the road to the park. The safest way to negotiate the tight, windy road to Manuel Antonio is by vehicle: either bus or taxi. Buses regularly transit between the Parque Nacional and the bus station in Quepos. Taxis can take us directly to hotels near the beaches in the area. However, from Quepos, we can also catch a bus back to San José. There are multiple departures throughout the day, and the ride is approximately 3 hours. In San José, the final stop is Bus Terminal Tracopa.

Sunset at the coast of the Pacific

Additional References

Accommodations vary along El Camino de Costa Rica. In some villages, the only lodging is with homeowners that rent rooms. Elsewhere, fancy hotels are adjacent to the trail. The locations listed here did not make deals or provide services in exchange for being mentioned.

It is wise to contact service providers in advance and make reservations before arriving at a destination. Regarding phone numbers: WhatsApp or other programs and tools are good substitutes for telephone service in Costa Rica. Unless otherwise specified, the country code / area code for phone numbers is +506. Businesses without a website or social media profile can often be found using travel service sites that facilitate recommendations online. If no contact information was available for a site, it was not included. Locations are listed alphabetically by section, followed by the community in which they are located, and the available contact information. All information is subject to change.

Resource Contact Information by Section

Section 1-A

-**Aventuras del Caribe.** Pacuare. Phone: 8725 4119 / 8621 3614. Facebook: Julio Knight.

-**Cabinas Iguana Verde.** Parismina. Phone: 2758 0224.

-**Green Gold Ecolodge.** Parismina. Phone: 8697 2322 / 8647 0691. Facebook: Green Gold Ecolodge.

-**Lirio Lodge.** Pacuare. Phone: 2282 5003. Facebook: Lirio Lodge. Web: http://www.liriolodge.com/

-**Parismina Gamefish Lodge.** Parismina. Phone: 2758 0724.

-**Rancho La Palma.** Parismina. Phone: 8550 7243.

-**Reserva Pacuare.** Pacuare. Phone: 4000 1557. Facebook: Pacuare Reserve. Web: https://www.pacuarereserve.org/

Section 1-B

-**Casa Araña.** Cimarrones. Phone: 8310 4142.

-**Casa Yolanda.** Cimarrones. Phone: 6325 1961.

-**Coast to Coast Adventures.** Pacuarito. Phone: 4001 2342. Web: https://www.coasttocoastadventures.com/

-**Hantarix.** Cimarrones. Phone: 2765 8025. Facebook: Hantarix Del Caribe.

-**Hotel Pacuare.** Siquirres. Phone: 2768 8111. Facebook: Centro Turístico Pacuare. Web: https://www.hotelpacuare.com/

-Rancho Rolo. Cimarrones. Phone: 5706 5542.
-Soda La Montañita. Cimarrones. Phone: 2765 8052.

Section 2

-Barbilla Rainforest Lodge. Las Brisas de Pacuarito. Phone: 8513 6982. Facebook: Barbilla Rainforest Lodge. Web: https://barbilla-rainforest-lodge.business.site/
-Escuela Brisas de Pacuarito. Las Brisas de Pacuarito. Phone: 2200 1774 / 8440 7639.
-Escuela Tsinikicha. Nairi Awari Indigenous Reserve. Phone: 8921 5016 / 8528 3475.
-Parque Nacional Barbilla Office. Las Brisas de Pacuarito. Phone: 2200 5224 / 8518 7802. Facebook: Parque Nacional Barbilla – SINAC. Web: https://areasyparques.com/areasprotegidas/parque-nacional-barbilla/

Section 3

-Casas Cosmogonicas. Tsiobata. Phone: 8504 3216.
-Indigenous Guides. Nairi Awari Indigenous Reserve. Phone: 8528 3475 (Clenet) / 8504 3216 (Leo). Email: adinairiawari@gmail.com

Section 4

-Cabañas El Paso del Viento. Tres Equis. Phone: 2554 1311. Facebook: Cabinas El Paso Del Viento.
-El Rancho de Cucho. Tres Equis. Phone: 2554 1017. Facebook: El rancho de cucho.
-Finca Tres Equis. Tres Equis. Phone: 8834 5199. Facebook: Finca Tres Equis. Web: https://fincatresequis.business.site/
-MegaSuper. Tres Equis. Phone: 2554 1591. Web: https://www.megasuper.com/
-Montañas del Pacuare. Tres Equis. Phone: 8483 6060. Web: https://montanasdelpacuare.com/
-Panadería y Repostería Alfa. Tres Equis. Phone: 2554 1491.
-Quijotes Bar Restaurant. Tres Equis. Phone: 2554 1441.

Section 5

-Casa y Comidas Rita. Pacayitas. Phone: 8622 7680. Facebook: Comidas Rita.
-Escuela San Pablo. San Pablo. Phone: 2554 1015.
-Finca Organica Cañaveral. San Pablo. Phone: 7012 6469. Facebook: Finca Orgánica Cañaveral.

-Finca ViaLig. Pacayitas. Phone: 8817 5330. Facebook: ViaLig Journeys.

-Hacienda la Corteza. San Pablo. Phone: 8821 5858. Facebook: Hacienda La Corteza CR.

-Super Salmerón. Pacayitas. Phone: 2531 5127. Facebook: Super Salmeron. Web: https://super-salmeron.negocio.site/

-Super de Pacayitas. Pacayitas. Phone: 2531 5031 / 2531 1333. Facebook: Supermercado Y Multiservicios Pacayitas.

Section 6

-Casa Nuñez Solano. El Silencio. Phone: 8588 6028.

-Siloe Lodge. Canadá de La Suiza. Phone: 8490 0664.

-Super Canada. La Canadá. Phone: 2531 1530.

Section 7

-Cabaña Margarita. Humo de Pejibaye. Phone: 8343 4309.

-Casa Hacienda Atirro. Atirro. Phone: 7017 6924. Web: https://casa-quinta-atirro.negocio.site/

-Casa Turire. Atirro. Phone: 2531 1309 / 2531 1111. Facebook: Casa Turire. Web: https://hotelcasaturire.com/

-Gerení Restaurant and Bar. Pejibaye. Phone: 7034 9325. Facebook: Bar & Restaurante Gerení.

-La Marta Wildlife Refuge. Pejibaye. Phone: 2542 0350. Facebook: La Marta Refugio de Vida Silvestre. Web: https://www.lamarta.org/

-Río del Valle Posada Turística. Pejibaye. Phone: 8707 5340. Facebook: Río del Valle Posada Turística.

Section 8

-Cabaña La Paz de Tausito. Tausito. Phone: 8896 4237.

-Casa Alex Smith. Taus. Phone: 8886 0885.

-Hacienda Ganadera. Purisil. Phone: 2533 9090. Facebook: Hacienda Ganadera Tapantí Media.

-Parque Nacional Tapantí Office. Orosi. Phone: 2206 5615. Facebook: Parque Nacional Tapantí Macizo de la Muerte. Web: http://www.sinac.go.cr/ES/ac/accvc/pntpmm/Paginas/default.aspx

-Refugio de Vida Silvestre El Copal. Tausito. Phone: 2531 2124 / 8880 0432. Facebook: El Copal. Web: http://elcopal.org/

Section 9

-Chalet Orosi. Orosi. Phone: 2533 3268. Facebook: Chalet Orosi. Web: https://chaletorosi.com/

-Finca Queveri. Orosi. Phone: 2200 4212. Facebook: Finca Queveri. Web: https://www.queveri.com/

-Green Mountain. Navarro del Muñeco. Phone: 8611 5253.

-Hacienda Orosi. Orosi. Phone: 2203 2265. Facebook: Hacienda Orosi. Web: https://haciendaorosi.com/

-Hotel Tapantí. Orosi. Phone: 2533 9090. Facebook: Hotel Tapanti Media de Orosi.

-Navarro Mountain. Navarro del Muñeco. Phone: 8425 3786. Facebook: Navarro Mountain Dream Renewed.

-Orosi Lodge. Orosi. Phone: 2533 3578. Facebook: Orosi Lodge. Web: https://www.orosilodge.com/

-Orosi Valley Hotels and Villas. Orosi. Phone: 4033 7599 / 8455 8509. Facebook: Orosi Valley Lodge.

-Rancho Río Perlas Resort and Spa. Orosi. Phone: 2533 3341. Facebook: Hotel Rio Perlas.

-Río Macho Lodge. Río Macho. Phone: 7282 5666 / 8392 3785.

-Soda Silvia. Navarro del Muñeco. Phone: 6354 8744.

Section 10

-Cabaña Camila: Quintas Palo Verde. Phone: 8585 2405.

-Palo Verde del Guarco Reserve (Bosque Nuboso Palo Verde). Palo Verde. Phone: 8928 1067 / 8822 1199 (Guides). Facebook: Bosque Nuboso Palo Verde.

-Verdesana Lodge. Palo Verde. Phone: 8313 5459. Web: http://verdesanacr.com/

Section 11

-Cabinas Turísticas Cerro Alto. Cerro Alto. Phone: 2571 1010. Facebook: Reserva Natural Privada Cerro Alto. Web: https://www.cabinasturisticascerroalto.com/

-Lubricentro. Cerro Alto. Phone: 6240 4030.

-Pulperia La Luchita. La Luchita. Phone: 6322 9916.

Section 12

-Albergue Cabo Luna: San Pablo de Leon Cortes. Phone: 8707 6776.

-Cabañas Bongos. San Pablo de Leon Cortes. Phone: 2546 5618. Facebook: Bongos Bar y Restaurante. Web: https://bongoscr.com/bongos/index.aspx

-Cabañas El Coyote. San Pablo de Leon Cortes. Phone: 8877 7824 / 8835 6021. Web: https://cabanas-el-coyote.business.site/

-Cabinas La Montaña. San Pablo de Leon Cortes. Phone: 8965 2314.

-Café Los Cuarteles. San Pablo de Leon Cortes. Phone: 8705 7430 / 8826 5245. Facebook: Café Los Cuarteles.

-Café Mutute. El Empalme. Phone: 2571 2323. Facebook: Mutute.

-Cafetería Los Chespiritos #3. El Empalme. Phone: 2571 1062. Facebook: Cafeterías Los Chespiritos. Web: http://chespiritos.com/

-Ecomiel (Honey Tour). San Marcos. Phone: 2546 7178 / 8843 5353. Facebook: Ecomiel. Web: https://eco-miel.com/

-Finca El Casquillo. San Pablo de Leon Cortes. Phone: 8384 2460. Facebook: Cultura Verde. Web: https://elcasquillo.wixsite.com/culturaverde

-Hotel Palenque Tarrazu. San Marcos. Phone: 8896 0356. Facebook: Hotel Palenque Tarrazu. Web: http://hotelpalenquetarrazu.com/

-Microbeneficio La Cabaña. San Pablo de Leon Cortes. Phone: 8340 3050. Facebook: Microbeneficio La Cabaña.

-Mirador El Jardín. El Jardin. Phone: 8305 5440 / 8753 9264 / 2546 1594 / 2571 1150.

Section 13

-Bar y Restaurante Mata de Caña Tarrazú. Mata de Caña. Phone: 2546 1312. Facebook: Mata de Caña Bar y Restaurante.

-Campamento San Gerardo. Iglesia Napoles de Tarrazu. Phone: 8436 7135.

-Estación de Servicio El Cruce. San Marcos. Phone: 2546 2565. Facebook: Estación de Servicio El Cruce.

-Finca Los Lirios. La Esperanza. Phone: 8317 7480. Facebook: Los Lirios.

-Pulpería La Flor. Mata de Caña. Phone: 2546 2969.

Section 14

-Campamento Naranjillo. Naranjillo. Phone: 8558 5726 / 2206 4203.

-Rancho Turistico Mirador Buena Vista Tarrazú. San Lorenzo. Phone: 8452 7986 / 8525 0743. Facebook: Rancho Turistico Mirador Buena Vista Tarrazú.

Section 15

-Chorro Ecolodge y H2O Adventures. Esquipulas. Phone: 8959 8989 / 8706 7458. Web: https://h2ocr.com/

-Esquipulas Bird Paradise Lodge. Esquipulas. Phone: 8382 1352 / 8871 1352. Facebook: Esquipulas Bird Paradise.

-Esquipulas Rainforest Lodge. Esquipulas. Phone: 8478 9556. Facebook: Esquipulas Rainforest.

Section 16

-Bar La Deportiva. Naranjito. Phone: 2779 1036.

-Best Western Hotel & Casino Kamuk. Quepos. Phone: 2777 0811 / 8787 1600. Facebook: Best Western Hotel & Casino Kamuk. Web: http://www.kamuk.co.cr/

-Blue Banyan Inn (BBI). Naranjito. Phone: 4070 0340. Facebook: Blue Banyan Inn.

-Cabañas y Piscina Villa Nueva. Villa Nueva. Phone: 8310 2760. Facebook: Cabañas y Piscina Villa Nueva. Web: https://cabanas-y-piscina-villa-nueva.negocio.site/

-El Gran Escape Restaurant. Quepos. Phone: 2777 7850. Facebook: El Gran Escape. Web: http://elgranescapequepos.com/

-Kids Saving the Rainforest (KSTR). Naranjito. Phone: 4070 0340. Facebook: Kids Saving the Rainforest. Web: https://www.kidssavingtherainforest.org/

-Marina Pez Vela. Quepos. Phone: 2774 9000. Facebook: Marina Pez Vela. Web: http://marinapezvela.com/

-Parque Nacional Manuel Antonio Office. Quepos. Phone 2777 5185. Web: http://www.sinac.go.cr/ES/ac/acopac/pnma/Paginas/default.aspx

-Serenity Boutique Hotel. Quepos. Phone: 2777 0572 / 8630 8997. Facebook: Serenity Boutique Hotel. Web: https://www.serenityhotelcostarica.com/

-Villa Vanilla. Villa Nueva. Phone: 8839 2721 / 2779 1155. Facebook: Villa Vanilla Spice Farm. Web: http://www.rainforestspices.com/

-Wide Mouth Frog. Quepos. Phone: 2777 2798 / 8550 8788. Facebook: Wide Mouth Frog Backpackers Hotel Quepos. Web: https://www.widemouthfrog.org/

Transportation Hubs

-Bus Terminal Tracopa. San José. Phone: 2221 4214 / 7298 3342. Facebook: Tracopa. Web: https://www.tracopacr.com/

-Juan Santamaría International Airport (SJO). Alajuela. Phone: 2437 2400. Facebook: SJO Aeropuerto Internacional Juan Santamaría. Web: https://sjoairport.com/en/

-Parada Alajuela. San José. Phone: 2442 6900 extension 125 & 126. Web: https://www.grupotuasa.com/index.html

-Terminal Caribeños. San José. Phone: 2222 0610. Web: https://centrocoasting.com/costarica/san-jose-gran-terminal-del-caribe/

Map List

About the Author

On his first attempt, without a GPS device, and accompanied only by a local guide when required in the indigenous territory, Evan Brashier completed El Camino de Costa Rica: the first known foreigner to do so. To achieve this, he relied on homemade maps built from online resources, a Spanish translation tool on his telephone, and the patience and kindness of the people of Costa Rica. He has since covered the trail multiple times in both directions, and significantly improved his Spanish language abilities. He wrote this book with the generous support of Asociación Mar a Mar, so that others could plan and complete their own independent crossings of El Camino de Costa Rica. His next project is establishing a home in Costa Rica with his fiancé, Isamar, whom he met while researching El Camino de Costa Rica, and without whose encouragement and patience this book may never have been finished.

The author in San José: December of 2019

Printed in Poland
by Amazon Fulfillment
Poland Sp. z o.o., Wrocław

27230447R00092